the Ultimate
CARDMAKER

180 CARD IDEAS AND
20 ESSENTIAL TECHNIQUES

David and Charles

A DAVID & CHARLES BOOK
Copyright © David & Charles Limited 2007

David & Charles is an F+W Media Inc. company
4700 East Galbraith Road, Cincinnati, OH 45236

First published in the UK in 2007
Reprinted 2007 (3 times), 2008, 2009
Text and photographs copyright © Crafts Beautiful 2007

Crafts Beautiful have asserted their right to be identified
as author of this work in accordance with the Copyright,
Designs and Patents Act, 1988.

A catalogue record for this book is available from the
British Library.

ISBN-13: 978-0-7153-2676-3 hardback
ISBN-10: 0-7153-2676-7 hardback
ISBN-13: 978-0-7153-2596-4 paperback
ISBN-10: 0-7153-2596-5 paperback

Printed in China by Shenzhen Donnelley Printing Company Ltd.
for David & Charles
Brunel House   Newton Abbot   Devon

Commissioning Editor Jane Trollope
Editor Jennifer Fox-Proverbs
Desk Editor Bethany Dymond
Proofreaders Helen Burge and Juliet Bracken
Production Editor Melissa Hyland
Art Editor Sarah Underhill
Design Assistant Emma Sandquest
Photography Paul Barker
Production Controller Bev Richardson

Visit our website at www.davidandcharles.co.uk

David & Charles books are available from all good
bookshops; alternatively you can contact our Orderline
on 0870 9908222 or write to us at FREEPOST EX2
110, D&C Direct, Newton Abbot, TQ12 4ZZ (no stamp
required UK only); US customers call 800-289-0963 and
Canadian customers call 800-840-5220.

Project Designers

Sharon Bennett studied graphic design and illustration, working as a packaging designer before going freelance in 1990. She has three books published by David & Charles, with a fourth due in 2007 and another in progress. She enjoys concept work, painting on ceramics and creating her own motifs.

Tracey Daykin-Jones has been making cards for five years and became involved with *Crafts Beautiful* after sending in two for the letters page. She was commissioned to design three more for a supplement and has since provided several more projects.

Glennis Gilruth has completed a degree in Surface Pattern. She enjoys sharing her knowledge and enjoyment of paper and fabric crafting with the readers of *Crafts Beautiful* and *Quick & Crafty!* She strives always to make her designs user-friendly and different, using a multitude of techniques and materials.

Brenda Harvey is a regular contributor to *Crafts Beautiful* and *Quick & Crafty!* magazines. A qualified teacher, she runs craft classes at sea for cruise passengers and also holds one-day workshops in the Midlands. Email her on brenda.harvey1@virgin.net.

Melanie Hendrick is a mixed media artist from Australia, now living in Scotland. She has two published card making books, designed a collection of scrapbooking papers and a rubber stamp range, and is regularly featured in craft magazines.

Julie Hickey is a successful card maker, workshop tutor and author. She is involved with running the Craftwork Cards Club, with over 7,000 members in the UK, USA and Europe. Her designs can be seen at www.craftworkcards.co.uk

Ellen Kharade originally trained as a stained glass designer, working as a glass conservator at Lincoln Cathedral for the past eleven years. She has moved into more craft-based work with a special interest in textiles, contributing regularly for *Crafts Beautiful* and *Quick & Crafty!*, and has written two books.

Jane Kharade has moved freely from one art form to another due to her strict training in stained glass. She says she cannot imagine doing anything other than being creative; from cards to jewellery, she enjoys the pleasure they bring her.

Elizabeth Moad has practised crafts for several years and regularly contributes to crafts magazines. She recently completed a BA degree in Fine Arts and is the author of *The Papercrafter's Bible* and *Cards for Lads and Dads*, from David & Charles.

Susan Niner Janes created best-selling Fold-It Swirls paper shapes for scrapbooking company Hot Off The Press. She is the author of eight craft books, including *Bright Ideas in Papercrafts* from David & Charles, and is a regular contributor to *Crafts Beautiful*.

Sally Southern has designed projects for several craft books and magazines and is

currently writing a book for David & Charles. She works as a freelance textile artist, and runs workshops for schools and youth groups.

Dorothy Walsh's stamping career has spanned over ten years. She has had work published in four UK, and four American magazines. She is a regular designer for *Crafts Beautiful* and enjoys teaching classes at her local stamp store.

Ruth Watkins hosts regular workshops at her Buckingham studio, Wooden-it-be-lovely. She has her own range of collage and scrapbooking papers, and is working on a book of pen and wash cards. For more details, call 01296 748683 or visit www.wooden-it-be-lovely.co.uk.

Karen Weiderhold has been crafting ever since childhood and has been scrapbooking and card making over the last six years. She loves running workshops, is a published designer and would like to write her own crafting book.

Janet Wilson has enjoyed crafts since early childhood, becoming proficient in a wide range of skills. She is best known for her love of and research into old paper arts from around the world and bringing them once more to the notice of modern day crafters.

Dorothy Wood is a craft designer and author with a contemporary approach. She studied Embroidery and Textiles at Goldsmith's Art College. Dorothy has written more than 20 books and regularly contributes to craft magazines.

Contents

Introduction

We all send lots of cards throughout the year, to mark a special occasion or to keep in touch with someone we love. Making your own special handmade card shows the recipient just how much you care and gives you so much pleasure, too. Cardmaking is relaxing, therapeutic and extremely rewarding, and you can achieve beautiful results with very little time and expense. It also gives you the opportunity to play around with colours and materials, experiment with different techniques and make the finished result look both personalized and highly professional.

Whether you are a beginner or an accomplished cardmaker, you are sure to be inspired by the wide range of cards and techniques featured in this book, presented by some of the world's top designers. There are so many techniques for you to try, from beading to rubber stamping, quilling to polymer clay. You will find practical advice and useful tips from the designers and it is easy to follow the step-by-step instructions to create the perfect cards to impress all your friends and family.

You might be surprised by just how quickly some cards can be made – you may even find that it is quicker to create a handmade card than to go out and buy one! Of course, there is no time limit and you may wish to spend more time and care creating a one-off card to commemorate a milestone event, which will be treasured for a long time by the recipient.

There are designs in this book to celebrate almost every card-giving occasion, from Christmas to Valentines, birthdays to wedding anniversaries. There are designs to please everybody, from children to grandparents, girly girls to the most macho of men and even those who are mad about pets! Feel free to change or adapt any of the card designs: add your own style, combine elements from several cards, but above all make them yours.

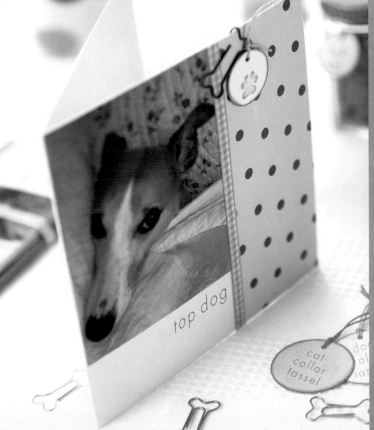

top dog

cat
collar
tassel

How to use this book

Pages 6–11 give you basic advice on the tools and materials
needed to make the cards in this book.

You will then discover a wealth of 180 beautiful cards. Each
of the twenty chapters introduces a different technique, which
is illustrated by a main card and followed by eight beautiful
variations, each giving you the chance to get plenty of practice
and perfect the techniques. Each card has a top tip to inspire
you and indicates how much time you will need to
put aside to make the card.

Finally, templates are provided at the back of the book to help
you achieve a perfect finish on many of the projects.

Basic Tool Kit

It is useful to gather together a basic tool kit before you begin to make your cards, as you will need this equipment again and again. Listed below are the basic items that are necessary for making cards – you might find that you already have some of these at home. You will also need a few additional items for each project, as well as the appropriate paper and card (see pages 8–9), and these are listed with the project instructions.

Pencil, eraser and sharpener: A simple lead pencil with a sharp point is essential for marking your card accurately. Always use a good, soft plastic rubber that does not smudge.

Scissors: You will need a large pair for trimming and a small pair for more intricate work.

Cutting tools: Always use a craft knife with a metal ruler – the knife can cut nicks in a plastic one, making it unusable. Replace the blades regularly, as a blunt blade will not leave a clean cut. A self-healing cutting mat is ideal as they are smooth, flat and are easier to cut on than other surfaces. It will also protect your work surface.

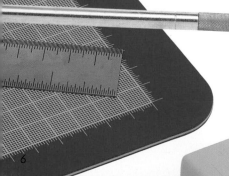

More Useful Tools...

Tweezers: These can be helpful for picking up small items.
Bone folder: This is useful for neatly creasing and folding card, scoring paper and smoothing creases.
Tracing paper: Use this for tracing the patterns and templates used in this book (see pages 252–254). Cheap copier paper can also be used.

Get Stuck in!

Different types of glue and adhesive are required in cardmaking for different purposes, so it is important to keep a range in your kit to achieve the best results.

PVA glue: Safe, inexpensive, all-purpose glue, which becomes transparent when dry.
Glue stick: Tubes of solid glue that can be rubbed over areas to leave a sticky residue, good for applying an even coat of adhesive.
Clear adhesive dots: These are perfect for sticking fiddly shapes to card. Place your item over the glue dots and firm down, so that the glue dots stick to them.
Adhesive foam pads: These are great for achieving a raised effect. They are adhesive on both sides – simply remove the backing paper and stick to the card or item.
Double-sided tape: This is quick and clean to use and is invaluable for adding layers to a design.

Colour and Embellishments

There is a huge range of decorative materials to choose from to add colour, textural and dimensional interest to your cards. Using a wide range of colour will really brighten up your cards and pretty embellishments always add that extra special touch.

Brads: These come in many different designs, including circles, squares, hearts and flowers. To attach, simply cut a slit in the card, push the brad through, turn the card over and open out the legs.

Eyelets: Use an eyelet punch, setter tool and hammer to attach eyelets. Working on a cutting mat, use the punch to create a hole in the card for the eyelet. Next, place the eyelet upside down and the card wrong side up and line up the hole with the eyelet. Use the setter tool to set the eyelet in your card.

Top Tip
Make sure your work surface is firm and steady when punching as some punches are quite stiff. You may need to stand up to apply more pressure to the punch.

Punches: These come in many different sizes to punch motifs into paper and lightweight card. They produce a shaped hole and a stamped shape, either of which can be used in your projects.

Colouring mediums: Pencils, chalks, paints, brush markers and felt pens are the main colouring mediums used in cardmaking. Each of these mediums can be used to create different effects. Experiment to find the ones you feel most comfortable using.

Rubber stamps and inkpads: There are thousands of stamp designs available and many different ways to use them to create quick designs that you can colour and embellish any way you please.

Peel-off stickers: These are so simple to use and come in a multitude of colours and designs. Simply peel an image off the sheet and stick it onto your card.

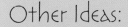

Other Ideas:

Glitter: This comes loose or pre-mixed with glue and is available in opaque and transparent colours. The finer the glitter, the better the transparency and coverage.

Embossing powders: To emboss, use a rubber stamp to stamp an image, apply the embossing powder, and then heat the powder using a heat tool. This creates a raised outline or surface on stamped images.

Ribbons: These can really add the finishing touch to your cards. There are so many different styles and sizes to choose from – plain, sheer, patterned, thin and wide.

Paper and Card

Paper and card are vital ingredients in cardmaking, and there is a wide variety to choose from, including plain, pearlescent, mirror, patterned, vellum, and many more. Go for the best quality you can find. Paper is sold in A4 sheets, in scrapbooking sizes – 12x12in or 8x8in pieces – or in pads of various sizes.

Look out for different finishes and patterns, some of which are illustrated below. Patterned papers are very popular and come in every design you can think of, suitable for many uses and occasions. A touch of shimmer can make a card special and an ornate card only needs a simple design to turn it into something stunning. Using different textures will also add interest and another dimension to your cards. Such an abundance of choice exists in terms of colour, texture, finish, weight and size that no two cards need ever look the same!

Vellum paper: A translucent paper with a smooth finish, available in a variety of colours, patterns and finishes, including embossed varieties.

Other Ideas:

Gift wrap: why not try using gift wrap, which is quite sturdy and comes in a wide range of patterns? Use the pattern as a decorative background or cut out individual motifs and use them as embellishments.

Mulberry paper: There are lots of fibres in this lovely handmade paper. Use a paintbrush to mark where you want to tear the paper, then tease the dampened fibres apart to create a delicate wispy edge.

Metallic foil: On these striking papers, the pattern has been applied with foil that resembles shiny metal. Pearlescent and shiny papers can be difficult to work with but give great results.

Handmade paper: These come in fabulous colours, but it is their different textures and surfaces that set them apart from machine-made papers. They often have natural elements, such as grasses, petals or leaves embedded in them, which makes them thicker than everyday paper.

Mulberry Paper

Patterned Paper Vellum

Patterned Paper Vellum

Handmade Paper

Metallic Foil

Card Blanks:

If you don't want to buy card and score it and fold it yourself, blank cards are available in many different colours, shapes and sizes and in different finishes: from plain to pearlized, patterned to textured. They are more expensive than buying card and scoring and folding it yourself, but you may decide they are worth the money for the crisp, clean look they produce. Card blanks with ready made apertures (see above) are also available, which have small shapes cut out of them in all sorts of sizes, including circles, squares, ovals and rectangles. These apertures are ideal for displaying small embellishments.

Storage:

A good storage system is essential for finding the paper and card you need, when you need it. Follow these tips to keep your paper and card easily accessible and in perfect condition.

Patterned paper: Store this in a folder (below) divided up into colour sections.
Scored and folded card: Organize your cardstock first by size, then by shape, colour, texture, aperture and so on.
A4 (US letter) card: Keep a store of various colours easily available for scoring and folding your own cards.

Top Tip
To give your cards the all-important professional finish why not embellish the envelope to match the card inside? This will create a wonderful first impression!

Envelopes:

There is a wide range of envelopes available to buy, in all sorts of colours and sizes. However, these are very easy to make yourself. Just look at an envelope and see how simply the shape is constructed. Always make sure the top flap is deep enough to allow you to seal the envelope without the glue touching the card inside.

Basic Techniques

As well as buying pre-cut card blanks, you will also need to make your own from a special piece of card. Uneven cutting can really stand out, and if you notice that something is not quite straight, then the recipient will too. Here are some simple papercrafting techniques that will ensure you produce professional-looking cards in next to no time. Follow these instructions for cutting, scoring and folding card, making card inserts for adding a special message inside, and using templates.

Scoring and folding: Scoring paper allows it to be folded neatly and easily, giving a crisp, professional looking finish.

1 Make two pencil marks where you want the score line on the wrong side of the card or paper and line up the ruler with these marks. Draw an empty ballpoint pen or scoring tool all the way along the line so the paper is indented. The scored line will become the inside of the fold.

2 Use both hands to fold the paper or card along the fold line. To make the fold line sharp, use either a bone folder on its side or the back of a clean metal spoon to press along the line.

Cutting: Make the cleanest cuts with a flat, clean surface, a sharp craft knife and metal ruler, and a steady hand.

1 Using an HB pencil and metal ruler, make two or three pencil marks on the card where you want the cutting line. With the card on a cutting mat, place the metal ruler along the line to be cut. It is best to stand when cutting with a craft knife. Put downward pressure on the ruler to hold it in place, while you draw the knife towards you in a single motion. Cut with the section you wish to use under the ruler, to ensure the knife will cut into the waste part if it slips.

2 Keep the blade of the craft knife at a 45-degree angle when cutting. Make sure you don't press too hard as you draw the knife across the paper, or it will wrinkle and leave an uneven edge. If you are cutting thick card or paper, draw the blade across once without too much pressure, then cut again with more pressure to make the final cut.

Top Tip

For larger sheets of paper or card, mark the cutting line with three pencil marks and cut about 20cm (8in). Keeping your knife in the paper, move your hand down the ruler, press firmly and continue cutting. Repeat several times using a long ruler.

Adding inserts: Adding an insert is a great way of adding a final, professional touch to your cards. They don't always have to be white or cream. You could try using papers in pastel shades or bright colours, patterned papers and pretty vellums. Inserts are another good way of adding decoration to your cards simply.

1 You can either use a paper trimmer or a craft knife, cutting mat and ruler, as explained on the previous page to cut your insert. First, measure the width of your folded card and subtract 5mm (³⁄₁₆ in) from it (W). Next, measure the height of the card and subtract 1cm (³⁄₈ in) from it (H). Fold the insert paper in half and crease well. Measure out from the fold and trim to W then measure up the fold and trim to H.

2 Apply 3mm (¹⁄₈ in) wide double-sided tape or a thin line of glue to the back of the folded insert along, but not over, the fold. Open the card and, keeping the distance between the top and bottom edges of the card equal, butt the insert up to the card fold. Press in place.

Using Templates: You will find templates for some of the shapes used in this book on pages 252–254. You can use some of these at actual size, but others will need to be enlarged on a photocopier set at 200% enlargement. It is very easy to use templates to copy an image that you might otherwise find difficult to scale up and draw. Follow the simple instructions below.

1 Use an HB pencil and tracing paper to trace the chosen image from the template, or photocopy the image onto paper. Cut around the image using scissors.

2 Place the paper template on scrap card. Hold the paper in place and draw around the paper template using a pencil.

3 Cut out the image from the cardboard to form the template. Discard the paper template, as this will not be sturdy enough. You can label and store your cardboard templates in plastic sleeves in a ringbinder for future use.

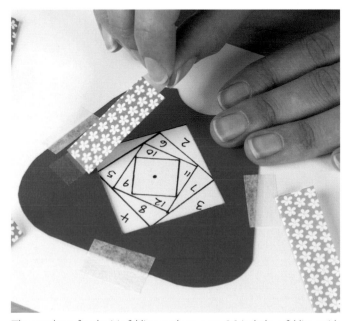

The templates for the iris-folding cards on page 36 include a folding guide which shows where to place your strips of paper and should be taped to scrap card so you can work over it.

Pretty Parchment

Create dainty greetings
on translucent parchment paper for a
really delightful result

Parchment craft is a delicate technique in which subtle white designs are drawn on specialist translucent paper with an embossing tool. These can be coloured in with ink or pens after. You can create different shades of white embossing by varying the pressure on the embossing tool. This historic technique is easy to master and can be as simple or as complex as you wish.

Pink Lady

This lovely card is perfect for a female relative or friend. Here the delicate flower design has been embossed and then coloured with orange and pink felt-tip pens. Gold highlights were added as a final sparkle.

1 Trace the flower and leaf outlines onto parchment paper using a sharp white pencil and the template on page 253. Once traced, place the parchment paper onto a dark-coloured foam pad with the pencil marks uppermost.

You will need

Parchment paper, 10cm x 13cm

Pink single fold card blank

Orange and pink felt-tip pens

Gold ink and a mapping pen

Foam pad

Four square pink brads

Mini hole punch

Medium and large ball embossing tools

White pencil

Eraser

TIME: One hour

PROJECT DESIGNER: Elizabeth Moad

Top Tip
When applying gold ink, shake the bottle well before use to ensure the colour is evenly distributed, and check the nib of your pen is clean.

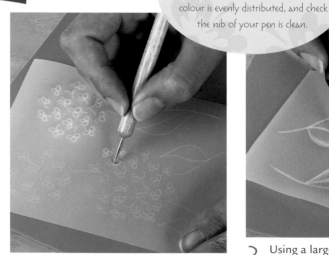

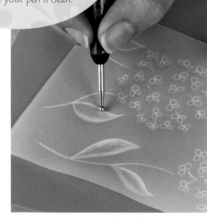

2 Go over all the pencil marks with a medium ball embossing tool, applying a steady, gentle pressure as you emboss. You may wish to practise first on scrap parchment to find the degree of pressure you need. Keep turning the paper over to check how the finished surface looks.

3 Using a large ball embossing tool go over the leaves, applying more pressure at the edges to produce a stronger shade of white. Turn the paper over so that the raised embossed side is now uppermost and keep on the dark pad so you can see the design clearly.

4   With a pink felt-tip pen, colour in all the petals on two of the flower heads, keeping within the embossed lines. Colour the petals on the remaining flower head with an orange felt-tip pen in the same way. Leave your parchment to dry for a few minutes.

6   Place the parchment paper over the front of the pink card blank and hold firmly in place. Using a mini hole punch, pierce a hole in each corner of the parchment paper, going through both the paper and the front of the pink card underneath.

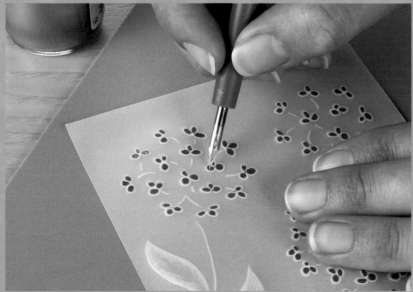

7   Push a pink brad into each of the holes you have just made from the front, going through both the paper and card. We used square brads, but round or shaped ones are suitable, too.

5   Take a mapping pen and dip it into the pot of gold ink. Add a dot of colour in the centre of each flower by lightly pressing the nib onto the paper. Shade in some of the petals in gold as well. See the main picture on page 13.

8   Turn the card over and splay the wings of each brad outwards with your fingers so that they lie flat against the back of the card. If any of the brads are showing on the front, move the ends around or trim them with pliers to hide them.

Mistletoe

This simple embossed parchment design for the festive season is made to look extra special by threading ribbon through holes punched in the turquoise card.

TIME: One hour
DESIGNER: Elizabeth Moad

Top Tip
Always keep your hands grease free when using parchment paper to avoid leaving marks on the paper.

1 Cut a square of parchment paper. Position over the template on page 253 and draw around using a white pencil. Place onto a foam pad with the pencil marks still uppermost.

2 Draw over the outline with a fine ball embossing tool before adding the berries with a medium tool. Press gently while the tool and paper warm up, then gradually apply more pressure to create a stronger image. Keep turning the paper over to see what the image looks like on the right side. Use an eraser to remove any visible marks.

3 Score and crease pearlescent blue card to make a single-fold blank. Attach the parchment diagonally to it with glue dots. Make two holes through the parchment and card, thread with pink ribbon and tie a bow. Punch holes in three corners of the card, thread ribbon through, and tape on the back.

On The Wing

Delicate butterflies and flowers cut from parchment paper and embellished with beads are used to create a card that's perfect for a summer birthday or anniversary.

TIME: One hour
DESIGNER: Jill Alblas

Top Tip
When tracing the template with white ink, take care to start at the top of the parchment and work down. This will cut down any smudging.

1 Fold 16cm x 15cm of pink parchment paper in half to measure 8cm x 15cm. Tape to the template on page 253 with the right-hand side of the folded parchment over the design. Trace over the lines with a pen and white ink. Turn the parchment over and emboss the petals with a medium embossing tool.

2 Use a pen and white ink to trace the two butterflies onto white parchment paper, then cut them out with paper scissors. Fold each butterfly carefully down the centre, apply glue down the fold, then stick them on top of the drawn butterflies on the front of the pink parchment.

3 Glue a line of pink rocaille beads down the centre of each butterfly, and more beads for their antennae tips and in the flower centres. Leave to dry, then fold the parchment over a tall, white card blank and tie with narrow ribbon.

1 Use a pen and white ink to draw a butterfly design and border onto white parchment paper. Turn the parchment over and emboss the antennae and the outline of the wings and body using a fine ball embossing tool.

2 Stick the parchment onto turquoise card and cut out leaving a narrow turquoise border showing around the parchment panel. Punch a hole in the centre top through both the parchment and card, and thread with white ribbon. Fold and crease a tall, light turquoise card blank, and pierce a hole in the centre top as well.

3 Glue the butterfly parchment panel 2cm up from the bottom of the light turquoise card blank. Thread the white ribbon through the hole at the top of the blank and tie in a bow. Glue a small pearl at the tip of each antenna and three oval pearls down the centre of the butterfly's body.

Holly Blue

A dainty butterfly motif drawn and embossed on white parchment paper and stuck to turquoise card makes a beautiful greetings card.

Top Tip
Use strong clear craft glue to stick the beads and press them down firmly with a tissue or piece of kitchen roll.

TIME: 40 minutes
DESIGNER: Jill Alblas

Winter Wonderland

This beautiful subtle winter design has a vellum panel embossed with delicate snowflakes and will make a gorgeous Christmas greeting.

Top Tip

Be careful not to overuse the rhinestone glitter – too much sparkle will overwhelm such a delicate card design and hide the embossed snowflakes.

TIME: 35 minutes

DESIGNER: Jo Gratwick

1 Score and fold an A5 white hammered card blank in half along the length and trim 3cm from the bottom. Tear off a 5cm strip of white vellum using a ruler. Emboss a snowflake border down the centre of the vellum using a Winter Wonderland Shapeboss template.

2 Turn the vellum over and apply accents to the design using rhinestone glitter. Leave to dry. Punch four snowflakes from mirror card and fix to the vellum with glue dots.

3 Place more glue dots on the reverse of the vellum underneath the mirrored snowflakes and adhere to the front of the white card blank. Tie a white satin ribbon, 3mm wide, around the fold to finish off your card.

Daisy Fresh

Make a special daisy greeting to brighten someone's day. The design is quick to make using easy layering and embossing techniques.

1 Crease and fold 28cm x 14cm of white card in half to form a card blank. Cut a 7.5cm square of gold mirror card, attach to the blank with 3D sticky foam pads and layer slightly smaller squares of white and lemon card on top of each other to create a gold and a white narrow border.

2 Draw a daisy-like flower using a large ball embossing tool on white parchment paper. Cut out around the outline. Apply yellow liquid appliqué to the centre of the flower.

3 Leave the appliqué to dry, then use a heat gun to puff it up. Attach the flower bloom to the centre of the layers on the card blank with a 3D sticky foam pad. Finish off by adding a length of lemon organza ribbon tied around the card spine.

Top Tip
To avoid splitting the parchment by embossing too heavily, 'sandwich' it between two thin sheets of paper before running through the machine.

TIME: 20 minutes, plus drying time
DESIGNER: Brenda Harvey

Heart of Gold

This elegant and romantic card trimmed with ribbon and beads is perfect for celebrating an engagement, wedding or anniversary.

Top Tip

If you stand up when using a border punch, you'll find it much easier to line up the pattern on the template.

TIME: 20 minutes
DESIGNER: Brenda Harvey

1 Crease and fold some A5 gold mirror card in half to form a card blank. Punch one edge of a 16cm square of white parchment paper with a flower border punch.

2 Position the parchment over the blank, slightly to the left of its right-hand edge and carefully score the central fold line. Fold the excess around the card spine and stick down on the back with double-sided tape.

3 Cut two gold card shapes using a heart punch of your choice, and attach them to the front of the parchment using 3D sticky foam pads. Tie some white organza ribbon around the spine and thread three small gold beads on to each end, tying a single knot to secure them in place.

1 Cut 15cm x 10.5cm of lime green floral scribble paper, and tear the right-hand short edge. Stick to a 14.5cm square white card blank. Keep the fold facing up and leave the lower half of the front panel uncovered.

2 Cut 15cm x 6cm of avocado self-adhesive vellum. Tear the top long edge and stick to the front of the card so that it covers half of the lime green paper. Use the torn-off strip to decorate the bottom edge.

3 Cut a flower from the lime green paper, stick to white card and trim the edges to leave a narrow margin all around. Fix in place with 3D sticky foam pads. Decorate the centre of the bloom and the lower left-hand corner of the card with self-adhesive crystal dots.

Green Daisy

Create a pretty and striking floral greeting in fresh shades of green and white, using easy layering techniques with a floral patterned paper and vellum.

Top Tip
The self-adhesive coloured vellum is easy to work with and subtly echoes the floral pattern.

TIME: 25 minutes
DESIGNER: Brenda Harvey

Winter Wishes

Capture the beauty of a winter wonderland with this snowflake embossed card made from translucent vellum using a brass stencil and embossing paste.

TIME: 20 minutes
DESIGNER: Paula Pascual

Top Tip
Embossing paste is ideal for creating snowflakes. Spread it over the brass template using a palette knife – just as if you were icing a cake.

1 Cut 11.5cm x 30cm of blue vellum card, crease and fold it in half. Stick down a brass stencil (Dreamweaver LJ819) on all four sides using low-tack tape. Apply a coat of white embossing paste over the stencil.

2 Carefully remove the tape except from three sides, and lift the stencil to check that all areas have been covered with the embossing paste. Apply some more paste if necessary then remove the tape completely. Sprinkle transparent glitter all over the card and shake off the excess.

3 Allow the vellum card to dry for 15 to 20 minutes (embossing paste drying times vary, so always check the instructions first). Stamp your message on some white card using a sepia ink-pad and trim the card down so that it is shaped like a ribbon. Attach your message to the card with a drop of PVA glue along the left edge.

Tea Time

Fold delicate papers to create beautiful shapes and patterns that are perfect for decorating cards

Tea bag folding is based on modular origami. The technique was invented by the leading Dutch origamist Tiny van der Plas in 1992 who used the gaily coloured envelopes from continental fruit tea bags, hence the name. Each rosette takes up to eight tea bag envelopes. Printed sheets of patterned 'kaleidoscope folding' squares are now widely available for cardmakers to use.

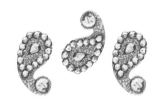

Taste of Darjeeling

This beautiful card uses just one of Tiny's folding techniques to create three different, intricate effects. The papers are decorated with a lovely Indian pattern – rather appropriate for a tea bag folded project!

You will need

Two sheets of tea bag papers

A4 emerald card

A4 emerald paper

PVA glue and cocktail stick

Paisley embellishment (optional)

Emerald jewel stone (optional)

TIME: One hour

PROJECT DESIGNER: Janet Wilson

1 Cut eight, 4cm squares from one sheet of tea bag paper. With the patterned side facing, fold and unfold each piece along the diagonal guide lines as shown in the diagram.

2 Turn over one paper square, then fold and unfold it along the horizontal and vertical guide lines, as shown in the diagram. Repeat on the other squares.

3 Push in the folds on the top right and bottom left corners. Bring the points to the bottom right corner. The top left one will automatically come down to this corner, creating a small square.

4 Turn the paper so the open points are at the bottom, and lift the top layer on the left-hand side. Fold inwards so that the outside straight edge sits against the central fold. Turn over and fold in the right-hand side. Flatten out.

5 Using the cocktail stick, dab a dot of PVA glue on the right-hand side of the fold. Slip the next element in by sliding the left-hand edge of it under the upper 'V' and matching the closed points (variation 1).

6 Make more folded sections, using eight, 5cm square papers, and apply glue as for step 5. This time the open points overlap and match up (variation 2).

7 Stick the completed tea bag fold from step 5 centrally onto the larger one in step 6, lining up symmetrically.

8 Cut the card and paper layers. Attach the corner-to-corner strip first, then the central square to the blank. Stick the double rosette onto the centre of the card and add embellishments to your taste.

Super Star

Fold beautifully decorated tea bag papers and put them together on a card to create this charming and intricate greeting that your family and friends will love.

Top Tip
Use a bone folder or burnisher to help with folding if you find a cocktail stick difficult to handle.

TIME: 40 minutes

DESIGNER: Corinne Bradd

1   Trim eight, 4cm squares of blue and pink tea bag paper. Fold into quarters pattern-side-out, and fold pattern-side-in on the diagonals. Allow each piece to naturally form a smaller square, then hold the cut edges at the bottom while folding under the sides on the top layer.

2   Interlock and glue the eight pieces together to create a star shape and fix to the centre of a 9cm square of white card. Take four, matching 5cm squares and fold in the opposite direction to create a triangle. With the point at the top, fold both front sides in half and flatten to form symmetrical tails.

3   Glue these four decorative pieces over the corners of the white square and fix to the centre of a 10.5cm square card blank. Fold the edges of a 4cm paper square under and stick to the middle of the star. Add a few dark blue diamantés to finish.

Fortune Teller

A school playground favourite – the fortune teller – is reinvented as an attractive flower motif for this greeting, but the paper folding technique remains the same.

TIME: 25 minutes

DESIGNER: Corinne Bradd

Top Tip

Make your own tea bag squares out of wrapping paper, background papers, or even rubber-stamp your own design using coloured inks.

1 Cut four, 4cm squares of yellow tea bag paper and four, 4cm squares of green tea bag paper. Fold, following the instructions in step 1 on page 26.

2 Interlock and glue the folded pieces together, alternating the points to create four yellow corners and four green ones. Make a fortune teller from another 4cm square by folding the corners to the middle twice with the plain side up, then flipping the square over and repeating. The final fold will make the corners pop out.

3 Glue the fortune teller flower to the centre of the assembled star and decorate with green gemstones. Make three more from matching 5cm squares. Fix a strip of corrugated card to a wider section of metallic handmade paper and stick down the centre of an A6 cream card blank. Glue the star and flowers centrally down the panel.

Royal Rosette

Simple tea bag folding is combined with an elegant ribbon tassel to make a card everyone will love. You can adapt it to suit any colour scheme or occasion.

Top Tip

It's a good idea to practise tea bag folding on squares of scrap paper first, to avoid wasting any of your precious printed papers.

TIME: 25 minutes

DESIGNER: Corinne Bradd

1 Snip six, 4cm squares of blue and purple tea bag paper. Fold into quarters, pattern-side-in and fold on the diagonals, pattern-side-out. Allow each piece to naturally form a triangle, then fold each side underneath to make a square. Open out the rear folds and flatten to form a house shape.

2 Glue the six pieces together to form a rosette and thread a large round brad through the hole in the centre. Fix double-sided tape inside the flat bottom of one of the folded squares, but do not remove the covering strip. Then cut eight or nine co-ordinating ribbons in varying widths and lengths.

3 Remove the tape backing and fix the ribbon ends into the base of the rosette. Trim the ribbons by snipping a 'V' into each end. Stick the rosette to the top of a tall, thin pink card blank. Hold some of the ribbon tails in place with pieces of tape.

Emerald Star

Create a beautiful star pattern using a green and yellow tile-effect tea bag paper, mount on emerald green card and finish off with two matching wire decorations.

TIME: 30 minutes
DESIGNER: Janet Wilson

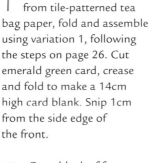

Top Tip

Fold each patterned square the same way. This way, the same part of the pattern appears at the front of the fold.

1 Cut eight, 4cm squares from tile-patterned tea bag paper, fold and assemble using variation 1, following the steps on page 26. Cut emerald green card, crease and fold to make a 14cm high card blank. Snip 1cm from the side edge of the front.

2 Cut a block of four, 5cm squares from the tile paper and glue centrally to the blank. Trim emerald green paper, 9.5cm square, and stick centrally to the first layer. Snip another block of four, 5cm squares, trim to 8cm square, and stick centrally to the emerald layer.

3 Cut a 7cm square of emerald green paper and glue to the middle of the last layer. Trim a 14cm x 1cm strip from the tile paper and stick to the card inside back edge. Stick the folded star shape in the middle and stick two ready-made wire embellishments on two opposite corners.

1 Cut eight, 4cm squares from 'points of view' tea bag folding paper, fold up and assemble using variation 2 following the steps on page 26. Cut a blank from blue card, 12.4cm x 17.6cm, crease and fold in half.

2 Cut a strip of the same tea bag paper, 17.6cm x 5cm. Trim another strip of blue paper or card, 17.6cm x 4cm, and stick centrally onto the patterned layer to leave a narrow border on either side. Stick this panel centrally to the card blank using double-sided tape.

3 Fix a compass clamp embellishment to the layered panel, 3cm up from the base of the card using glue dots. Stick the folded tea bag paper star 3cm from the top edge of the strip using 3D sticky foam pads.

Compass Points

This fun card is an ideal design to make for a keen hiker or intrepid traveller! It's created from a 'points of view' tea bag paper, and has a gorgeous compass embellishment.

Top Tip
You can easily choose a different theme for your greeting from the fantastic selection of tea bag papers and embellishments on offer.

TIME: 20 minutes
DESIGNER: Janet Wilson

Lucky Coin

The edges of the peony paper used on this gorgeous oriental-style greeting were trimmed into flower shapes, and the tea bag fold is set on acetate to look like it's reflected in water.

TIME: 40 minutes
DESIGNER: Janet Wilson

Top Tip
Use a new blade and a self-healing cutting mat when cutting around the peony flowers.

1 Cut eight, 4cm squares from Chinese peony paper, fold and assemble using variation 1 following the steps on page 26. Cut along the outline of each piece first. Cut the centre, second and third flower layers from three more squares and stick to the middle of the tea bag fold with sticky foam pads.

2 Cut a 7cm diameter circle from Chinese peony paper. Stick onto a blue card blank, 11.1cm x 21cm, 2cm from the top. Trim a 6cm diameter circle centrally into the paper circle, through the blank. Attach clear acetate, 8cm square, behind the aperture. Snip another flower layer and fix this to the back of the tea bag fold, then glue to the centre of the acetate.

3 Fix a Chinese coin 1.5cm below the aperture. Pierce a hole in the centre and thread a ready-made tassel. Tape on the back.

Eastern Promise

Indian patterned papers are ideal for tea bag folding – especially when you set them against an emerald green card blank. This design will make a fun introduction to tea bag folding.

TIME: 30 minutes
DESIGNER: Janet Wilson

1 Cut eight, 4cm squares from Indian-style tea bag paper. Fold and assemble variation 2 following the steps on page 26. Make four corner variations from squares of the same size. Cut an emerald green card blank, 14.6cm square. Cut gold paper, 11.5cm square, and stick to the centre of the emerald blank.

2 Trim the following layers of paper or card, and stick each one on top of the other, but do not affix to the blank yet: Indian paper, 11cm square; gold paper, 10.5cm square; green paper/card, 10cm square; Indian paper, 8cm square; gold paper, 7.5cm square; green paper/card, 7cm square.

3 Place a folded corner variation in each corner of the layered panel and secure in place. Stick centrally onto the gold panel on the front of the card blank. Finally, fix the tea bag fold to the middle of the top layer using 3D sticky foam pads.

Diamond Geezer

Diamanté gems add the finishing sparkle to this dainty flowered greeting made using leaf patterned paper and both variations from the steps on page 26.

from the steps on page 26.

Top Tip

Use different coloured or different shaped diamanté jewels to vary the overall effect of the card.

TIME: 45 minutes
DESIGNER: Janet Wilson

1 Cut eight, 5cm squares from leaf aurora tea bag paper, fold and assemble using variation 2 from page 26. Fold another eight, 4cm squares, this time using variation 1 from page 26. Trim round the leaf-shaped edge of each piece before assembling.

2 Cut a blue card blank, 14.5cm square. Layer purple tea bag paper, 10cm square, with blue paper, 9.5cm square, and stick to the middle of the blank.

3 Stick the variation 2 tea bag fold to the middle of the blue layer. Fix the trimmed variation 1 piece on top, points towards the valleys on the layer below. Glue a 5mm flat-backed diamanté in the centre, and eight more around the tea bag fold as shown.

Intricate Irises

Arrange patterned paper strips within
aperture cards to create an amazing effect

Iris folding is a fascinating papercraft technique
that originated in the Netherlands. Originally
the strips used were cut from printed envelope
linings, but now crafters can choose from beautiful
scrapbooking or origami papers. To create the
design, the lengths are arranged in spiral formation
behind a card aperture. The opening at the centre is
like the iris of the eye – hence the craft's name.

Fan Dance

Iris folding looks complex – but
appearances are deceptive. These
Japanese-style cards are surprisingly easy
to craft, and the simple patterns provide
an enjoyable introduction to this
beautiful technique.

You will need

20 x 20cm paper pack in citrus shades

A4 card in pinkish red, pearlescent turquoise and pearlescent gold

Decorative brads

Gold craft thread

Paper punches: 2cm flower, 1cm flower, and a needle for piercing a 2mm hole

Ruler-type paper-tearing tool

Rub-down adhesive

Low tack masking tape, double-sided tape and frosted cellophane

Double-sided 3mm sticky foam pads

Scissors and craft knife

Self-healing cutting mat

Metal ruler

TIME: 40 minutes

PROJECT DESIGNER: Susan Niner Janes

CIRCLE FAN

Refer to the pattern provided. Form the aperture with a circle-cutting tool. Use the colour key provided. The design is worked using the same method as for the square aperture card.

Top Tip

Trim the paper strip ends closely – you will be able to follow the pattern more easily and the resulting design will be crisper.

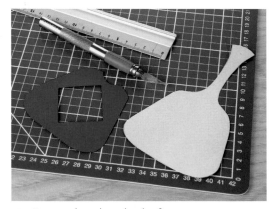

1 From red card, make the fan top with the square opening using the template on page 252. Cut out the window first (using a craft knife and ruler), then the fan outline. Create the paddle-shaped fan in gold card.

2 Trim strips from different coloured papers, by snipping the 20 x 20cm sheets in half, then dividing them into 3cm wide sections. Fold each in half lengthwise. Use scissors rather than a craft knife – only the folded edge shows in the final design, so precision cutting is not essential.

3   Photocopy the fan template, then cut out the iris folding pattern in the centre, with a margin around it. Tape the design onto scrap card or your work surface. Lay the fan cut-out over the pattern, wrong side facing upwards and fix in place.

6   Pierce a 2mm hole in gold card with the needle. Cut a small square, with the hole in the centre, to fit over the 'eye' of the iris pattern. Tape the card in place on the wrong side of the design. Remove the fan from your work surface.

4   Take a strip and tape in place over area 1, with the folded side facing inwards. Trim each end to extend 6mm beyond the marked area and secure with a tiny piece of tape. Refer to the key provided for the colours to use in each area.

7   Punch a small flower with a central hole from patterned paper. Thread onto a brad and fix in the middle of the iris. Pierce a hole at the end of the fan handle. Loop thread through and tie a flower on each 'tail'. Knot underneath and trim the ends.

5   Take the next paper and tape it onto area 2. Strips 3 and 4 complete the first round (of three). Stick two more rounds in this way until you have completed the pattern with area 12.

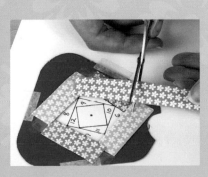

8   Cut 21cm x 20.8cm of turquoise card and fold. Tear a 4cm strip of patterned paper, and fix onto the fold side of the blank. Stick the gold fan to the blank with double-sided tape and mount the iris fold fan with sticky pads. Decorate with punched flowers.

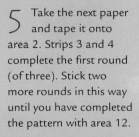

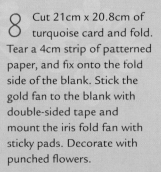

Pretty Patchwork

Create a delightful greetings card using iris-folding in a log cabin patchwork pattern. It's fun and easy to make, using the template on page 252.

1 Cut out a window frame in navy card, pinking the edges. Snip a small navy square for the iris. Cut 12, 2.5cm x 7cm strips from origami paper and fold each one in half lengthwise. Use contrasting paper colours and patterns, and position matching strips opposite each other to create a log cabin effect.

2 Tape the template onto scrap card, then the window frame, face down, on top of it. Fasten the strips as numbered, working from the outside inwards, then secure the iris in place (see page 39)

3 Use foam sticky pads to fix the iris motif onto an A6 card blank, tilted as shown. Glue two punched hearts onto the navy frame and a criss-cross paper strip 'kiss' onto the card as shown.

Top Tip
Iris folding is a great way of using up odd scraps of paper – clashing patterns can create some stunning effects!

TIME: 30 minutes

DESIGNER: Susan Niner Janes

Trim the Tree

Whip up this fantastic Christmas tree greeting in no time at all using a simple iris folding technique, and decorate it with festive coloured brads.

TIME: 30 minutes

DESIGNER: Susan Niner Janes

Top Tip

You can scale the template for this design down using a photocopier, if you want to make a smaller card.

1 Cut enough 1cm x 7cm strips of silver and green card for the template on page 252. Then cut a triangular window in red card. Snip zig-zag edges on two sides of the red window card, as shown. Tape the guide from the template onto scrap card and the triangle window, face down, on top.

2 Fasten the strips in place as explained in the steps on page 39, working from the top of the tree down to the base, using alternate colours. When the pattern is complete, pierce a hole at each marked dot with a needle, placing a putty eraser underneath the card to receive the tip.

3 Insert a large star brad at the top of the tree, and red and gold round brads in the holes as shown. Attach the red card onto an A6 silver card blank with foam sticky pads. Insert more brads in the lower corners of the card, as shown.

Floral Display

Make this delightful iris folded hexagon flower card trimmed with contrasting brads as a fun birthday greeting for a friend.

Top Tip
Origami paper is light and has no grain, making it perfect for folding and lying flat.

TIME: 30 minutes

DESIGNER: Susan Niner Janes

1 Using the template on page 252 as a size guide, draw then cut a six-sided scalloped 'window' in reversible paper. Lightly score the base of each petal and fold back the flaps to form a hexagonal window. Use low-tack masking tape to stick the petals flat.

2 Tape the iris-fold guide from page 252 onto scrap card and the petal window, face down, on top. Cut 3cm x 7.5cm strips from three colours of wave-pattern origami paper. Fold each one in half lengthwise and tape down as numbered (see page 39). The spiral pattern can be three or four rounds – snip the centre iris card to fit as necessary.

3 Pierce a hole in the central iris and insert a punched flower fixed with a brad. Cut a 25cm x 12.5cm contrasting card blank and fold in half. Fix the iris medallion, centred, onto the front. Pierce a hole in each corner and fix a brad.

Classical Style

Create a beautiful, earthenware style greeting using contrasting papers in rich shades of terracotta and gold. The papers are taped to the back of a vase aperture cut in the card.

TIME: 20 minutes
DESIGNER: Corinne Bradd

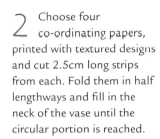

Top Tip

Always use a vivid or contrasting colour in the centre of an iris fold design to draw the eye.

1 Fold and score ribbed cream card to make an A6 blank. Draw a vase shape with a circular bowl in the centre of the inside front. Carefully cut out with a scalpel and lay flat, so that the inside is uppermost and can be worked on.

2 Choose four co-ordinating papers, printed with textured designs and cut 2.5cm long strips from each. Fold them in half lengthways and fill in the neck of the vase until the circular portion is reached.

3 Use a circular iris fold template to fill in the bowl. Tape the strips down carefully as explained on page 39, using the same colour sequence in each round. Attach a square of textured gold card face down over the centre of the pattern. Turn your card over and fix a small cream circle in the middle of the gold card. Punch several small circles from gold card to finish off the card.

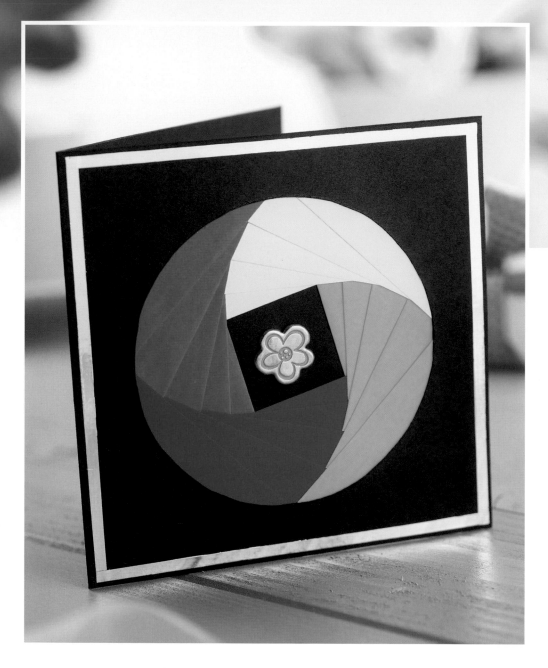

Neon Bright

Acid shades of pink, green and yellow paper teamed with black and silver make for a striking, modern iris folding design suitable for every occasion.

1   Cut a 3.5cm diameter circle from the centre of a black card blank, 10.5cm square. Edge the blank with 3mm wide silver tape, positioning it 1mm from the edge then trim neatly at the corners.

2   Cut 2.5cm strips of neon paper in four contrasting colours and fold each one lengthwise. Tape a circular iris fold template to fit the card aperture onto scrap card and the card blank on top. Fasten the strips in rounds starting from the outside and using the same colour sequence throughout (see page 39).

3   Position a piece of black card over the centre square of the design. Turn the card over and add a silver flower brad in the centre of the design to finish.

Top Tip
To get an extra-sharp fold, use a pin and a ruler to lightly score the paper before folding

TIME: 20 minutes
DESIGNER: Corinne Bradd

Indian Prints

Let the Far East be your inspiration for this bold, hexagonal greeting made from handmade Indian print paper in contrasting shades of pink and mauve.

Top Tip
Cut a hexagon template from thin card and draw round lightly to make your card aperture.

TIME: 20 minutes
DESIGNER: Corinne Bradd

1 Cut a 6cm wide hexagon from the middle of a 10cm square of bright pink card. Trim six types of decorative, Indian handmade paper into 1cm wide strips. Do not fold in half as this will make the pieces too thick.

2 Use a hexagonal iris fold pattern to fill in the aperture and stick a square of contrasting paper over the remaining hole. Turn the card over and trim into a hexagon shape, following the aperture and leaving a 1.5cm wide border.

3 Mount this panel onto darker pink card and trim a 3mm border around it. Glue the hexagon to a purple blank and trim the points of the shape with small round and tear-drop shaped gemstones.

Pentagon Pattern

Combine dark and light shades of blue to create a wonderful greetings card for a man. Clever effects can be achieved by using different textures as well as colours.

Top Tip

Lay your papers out next to each other to see the different combinations you can create with them.

TIME: 20 minutes

DESIGNER: Corinne Bradd

1 Cut a pentagon with 4.5cm long sides from the centre of white card, 10cm square. Trim 2.5cm strips from five patterned papers in shades of blue. Fold them all lengthways and arrange in order from dark to light.

2 Fill the aperture using a pentagonal iris fold guide, making the darkest strips form the outer ring. Progress towards the middle adding lighter strips each round. When you have used your palest shade, work the colour order in reverse, and use the darkest tone to cover the centre hole (see page 39).

3 Trim the white card, 1cm from the edge of the aperture and mount with 3D tape onto an A5 blank, covered with pale woven-effect paper. Mount a 1cm wide strip of mid-tone paper onto white card with a 1mm border and fix a silver star to the middle with a white mini brad. Fix centrally under the pentagon.

Floral Fantasy

Girls will love this pretty floral iris fold card. It's fun and easy to make using gorgeous papers in shimmering shades of pink and yellow and contrasting patterned card.

Top Tip

Use a craft knife and self-healing craft mat to cut sharp lengths when the papers are left unfolded.

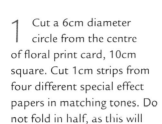

TIME: 20 minutes

DESIGNER: Corinne Bradd

1 Cut a 6cm diameter circle from the centre of floral print card, 10cm square. Cut 1cm strips from four different special effect papers in matching tones. Do not fold in half, as this will make the lengths too thick.

2 Place the floral print card face down over an oval iris fold pattern. Centre the middle diamond shape in the circle. Fill in the design by taping the strips in rounds, using the same colour sequence. Place a square of floral card over the centre.

3 Turn the card over and outline the circle edge with a decorative peel-off border coloured with permanent marker. Mount the floral square onto pink card leaving a 1mm border, and glue onto a yellow card blank, 13cm square.

Terrific Transfers

Create simple and effective card designs with ready-to-use transfer images

If you find drawing or painting your own designs for cards too tricky or time-consuming, help is at hand with transfers. They are so easy to use, yet the final result is very professional. They take the form of rub-down images, plus lettering and numbers, or you could even create your own from favourite photographs or pictures, with the aid of transfer paper.

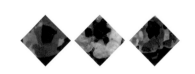

Remembrance Day

Create this unusual greeting using transfer paper designed for fabric, and a home computer. Images of poppies taken with a digital camera were ironed onto white felt, and turned into panels that look wonderful viewed through apertures cut into the card.

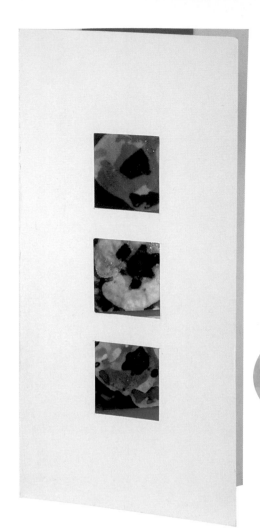

Top Tip
Make transfer paper go further by printing all the images onto one sheet

1 Edit a digital poppy photograph in Photoshop. Reduce it down to 4cm square. Select Filter and Artistic, from the toolbar. Create three images in 'water-colour', 'paint daub' and 'cut-out' and save each one. Print onto the transfer paper.

You will need
White felt

Transfer paper

White, orange and tangerine card

Poppy image

Glitter glue

TIME: 30 minutes

PROJECT DESIGNER: Jane Kharade

2 Iron the three images onto white felt, placing them paper side up and using a medium to high setting, with no steam. There are different transfer papers suited to light or dark materials; make sure you use the right one. Cut out all three and put to one side.

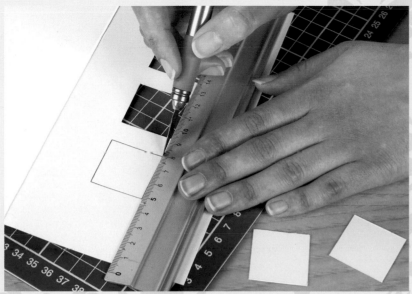

3 Score and fold a 21.5cm square of white card to form a long, tall card
  blank. Cut three apertures, 3.2cm square with a sharp craft knife on a
cutting mat. They should be spaced equally down the centre of the panel,
5cm from the top and bottom of the blank.

4 Cut 4cm x 16cm of tangerine card and
  5cm x 21cm of orange card. Stick the tangerine
panel on top of the orange one, then attach both
layers to the inside of the blank, down the middle
and in line with the apertures.

5 Stick the three poppy images centrally down
  the orange panel with double-sided tape.
Make sure that each of the flowers is lined up with
an aperture, so that they show through when the
card is closed.

Top Tip
As all photographic artwork is
original and your own, you can
use it on everything!

6 Finish off by adding
  highlights to the three
poppies with glitter glue. Apply
sparingly, perhaps just to the
darker areas of the image, or
wherever the light would fall on
the petals, to make them stand out.

Beach Comber

Transform a favourite seaside find into a lovely original greeting, simply and effectively using the software on a digital camera or computer.

1 Take a photograph of a nautilus shell, or other found object of your choice, using the Macro facility on a digital camera. Using the software with your camera or Photoshop on a computer, edit the image so that it measures 8.3cm x 11.5cm.

2 Print the shell image out onto transfer paper. Stretch an A5 sheet of decal-edged water-colour paper. Once dry, brush with diluted PVA glue and let it dry. This will protect your card and make the image shine.

3 Cut out the image and soak in a shallow dish of water. Release the transfer slightly from the backing paper and feed onto the water-colour paper, pressing out any air bubbles to ensure the image is flat. Leave to dry, then fold the card in two.

Top Tip
Practise printing your image onto standard A4 white paper before you use up a valuable sheet of transfer paper.

TIME: 35 minutes
DESIGNER: Jane Kharade

All Heart

Offer someone a soft and gentle token of love that's just a little different. A pebble painted with a white heart formed the basis for the transferred image in this unusual greeting.

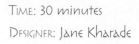
Top Tip
This unusual card would be ideal for many occasions; try changing the colours to suit another theme or painted image.

TIME: 30 minutes
DESIGNER: Jane Kharade

1 Edit a Macro photograph of a painted pebble or other found object to 8cm x 6cm, using the software from a digital camera or Photoshop on a computer. Print the image onto transfer paper for light fabrics. Iron the picture (paper side up) onto white felt.

2 Peel away the backing from the transfer paper. When the image has cooled, trim away the felt. Cut a blank from black card, 15cm x 10.5cm.

3 Tear two layers of white fibre paper, 9cm x 15cm and 6cm x 5cm, dampening it with a wet paintbrush first. Stick the white fibre paper onto the blank with a layer of black card in between. Attach the pebble image to the fibre panel with sticky foam pads.

Sheer Delight

Create a delicate, translucent design
that reveals the natural beauty of flowers
by transferring a photograph onto
flimsy white fibre paper.

1 Take a photograph of a pink gerbera, or similar flower, with the Macro facility on a digital camera. Using the accompanying software on your camera or Photoshop on a computer, edit the image to measure 8cm x 6cm.

2 Print out the picture onto transfer paper for light fabrics. Iron the flower (paper side up) onto white fibre paper. Peel away the transfer paper backing when cool and trim the image down to measure 6cm square.

3 Fold a 15cm x 21cm white card blank in half. Cut pink patterned paper, 8cm square, and fix it centrally to the blank with double-sided tape. Finish by attaching the flower image centrally to the pink panel.

Top Tip
Experiment with other types of flowers for this project – flat round varieties work best.

TIME: 25 minutes

DESIGNER: Jane Kharade

Fairytale Castle

Create a reminder of special holiday moments, with a romantic, vintage-style greeting made by transferring a holiday snap onto water-colour paper and fitting it in a card aperture.

TIME: 25 minutes
DESIGNER: Jane Kharade

Top Tip
Find a setting on your printer that applies as little ink as possible (i.e. transparency setting) when printing onto inkjet transfer paper because it is highly absorbent.

1 Take a favourite holiday snap and edit it into a black and white image, 8cm x 6cm, using your digital camera software or Photoshop. Print onto transfer paper, cut out and allow to dry. Soak in a shallow dish of water.

2 Release the transfer slightly from the backing and feed onto water-colour paper, which has been brushed with diluted PVA glue and left to dry. Press out any air bubbles. When no longer damp, trim and stick onto an A4 sheet of black paper.

3 Cut a 9.5cm x 5.5cm aperture from a white card blank, 15cm x 21cm. Carefully trim the black paper, so the image fits snugly in the aperture.

Blow the Candles

Turn a birthday party snap into a tasty-looking greeting when it's someone else's turn to celebrate. The image looks superb printed onto acetate.

1 Photograph a cup cake or similar piece of food, using the Macro facility on a digital camera. Edit the image to 8cm x 6cm with the accompanying software or Photoshop. Print out onto transfer paper.

2 Cut out the picture, allow to dry, then soak in a shallow dish of water. Release the transfer slightly from the backing paper and feed onto acetate. Press out any air bubbles. Fold a white card blank, 10cm x 29.5cm, in half and cut a 5cm x 7.5cm aperture with a craft knife.

3 Apply a continuous glue line on the underside edge of the image and attach to the aperture. Finish off by lining the inside of the card with pink paper, and adding your message above and below the aperture.

Top Tip
Soak the transfer in warm water to prevent the edges curling up when applied onto the acetate.

TIME: 30 minutes
DESIGNER: Jane Kharade

Bonus Print

Silver braid makes the perfect frame for this stunning greeting made by transferring a close-up photo of a favourite flower onto plain fabric and mounting it on matching pink card.

Top Tip
To use your transfer paper economically, when printing out smaller images, cut it into photograph-sized sheets.

TIME: 45 minutes

DESIGNER: Ellen Kharade

1 Take several digital shots of flowers and save them onto your computer. Select one and print it onto a sheet of transfer paper for textiles. Leave to dry for 30 minutes, then iron face down onto a small rectangle of white cotton.

2 Trim pink card, 13cm x 20cm and fold it in half. Cut stiff card, slightly smaller than your motif. Place a few strips of double-sided tape onto the front and back of the card and stick on the fabric, smoothing out any wrinkles.

3 Fold the excess fabric around the back. Fix in place on the front of the pink blank. Snip a few strips of decorative braid or ribbon and glue in place as a frame around the motif.

Fine Vintage

Rub-on initials give cards a professional touch and are ideal for making a personalised greeting, especially when combined with ribbons and lace.

1 Cut and fold A5 cream card to A6 size. Tear a strip of script-printed paper in muted tones and glue to co-ordinating, but plainer, patterned paper. Trim the panel to 9.5cm x 13.8cm and stick to the centre of the card blank.

2 Lightly stick antique lace along the bottom of the card, then stick three lengths of ribbon down the left-hand side of the paper panel. Decorate the ribbons with an assortment of metal charms and paper fasteners.

3 Position a decorative initial letter transfer, 3cm square, on the card off-centre, so that it overlaps both types of paper. Carefully rub the transfer onto the paper with a lolly stick tool, ensuring that all parts of the design have been transferred.

Top Tip

If you don't have a lolly stick tool, the blunt end of a pencil will work just as well for rubbing down a transfer.

TIME: 20 minutes
DESIGNER: Corinne Bradd

Shell Like

Combine rub-on transfers with 3D embellishments to make a stunning, tactile card like this pretty shell greeting trimmed with beads and real shells.

Top Tip
If you miss transferring part of the design, reposition the sheet over the design you have applied, and rub the rest in place.

TIME: 30 minutes
DESIGNER: Corinne Bradd

1 Cover an A6 card with lilac marbled paper and trim all edges neatly. Fix a strip of wide grosgrain ribbon down the left-hand side of the blank and hold in place with small brads.

2 Carefully rub five, coloured shell transfers onto the strip of ribbon, spacing them evenly down the length. Ensure all pieces of the design are stuck to the ribbon before lifting away the backing sheet.

3 Thread assorted seed beads and pearls onto thread and knot at the end. Glue the knot inside a small shell coloured with rubbing wax. Fix several of these bead chains to the front of the card with a brad as shown, then glue pearls and round glass beads around it.

Marvellous Modelling

Use polymer clay to create your own beautiful card decorations

While there are many lovely embellishments for greetings available, you can also create your own with the aid of polymer clay. This modelling material is so versatile, coming in a wide range of colours that can be mixed to create further shades. It is easy to sculpt and lightweight, making it perfect for decorating cards, plus you can harden it in your own oven.

Queen of Hearts

The pretty pale shades of clay used for this project were achieved by mixing other colours together. A pair of cookie cutters are all you'll need to model the heart shapes required – simple, yet effective.

You will need

Cognac, raspberry, blue, yellow,
white and turquoise Fimo clay

Cream and pink decorative card

Heart-shaped cookie cutters, large and small

Double-sided tape

PVA glue

Cutting mat

Scalpel

Metal ruler

TIME: 40 minutes

PROJECT DESIGNER: Ellen Kharade

Top Tip
If the clay becomes too soft to work with, pop it into the fridge for 15 minutes until it becomes firm.

1 Mix up a ball of white and cognac clay with a little yellow, until you have a pale biscuit colour. Repeat with an amount of white and a little blue to create pale turquoise.

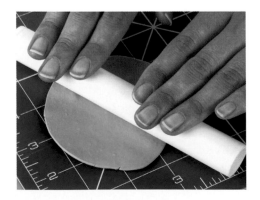

2 Make up a pale pink shade, by moulding white clay into a little raspberry. Using a small rolling pin, flatten the biscuit colour until it is 2mm thick. Press out three shapes, with the large heart-shaped cookie cutter.

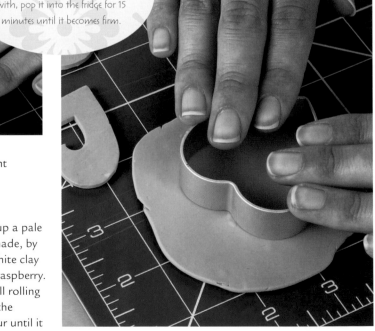

3 Take out the centres of each of the large hearts, using the smaller cutters and decorate with a tiny ball of raspberry clay. Put the little hearts to one side.

4 Roll out a long, thin sausage of pale pink and carefully run it along the edge of the heart. Press it down lightly to make sure that it has adhered to the base clay. Roll out small balls from pale pink, and dot them along the heart. Do the same with more spots from the raspberry colour.

7 Cut a strip of decorative paper, 8cm x 16cm and a rectangle of pink card, 5cm x 16cm.

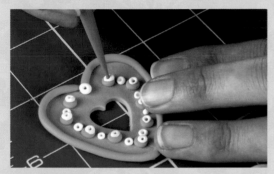

5 Make another raspberry and pink heart in the same way, then two more hearts, altering the colour scheme to turquoise and white. Press an old biro into each ball to make an interesting pattern.

6 Put all of the shapes carefully onto a baking sheet and place in the oven for 30 minutes at 130°C. Trim cream card, 16cm x 22cm, score and fold in half.

8 Place a few strips of double-sided tape onto the backs of the decorative paper and card, then stick one on top of the other. Glue the hearts into place with a few spots of PVA adhesive.

love blossoms

Shoots to Thrill

Let someone know you care by making this springtime bluebell card for them, and add your own special message using an eyelet message.

Top Tip
Sculpey polymer clay can be bought from most good craft shops and is ideal for these designs

TIME: One hour, with baking time
DESIGNER: Jill Alblas

1 Fold a white A5 card in half. Cut some lilac card, 7.5cm x 6cm, and glue onto the front of the white blank, leaving a gap of 2.3cm at the bottom. Fix an eyelet phrase in the centre, just below the coloured card. Put the blank to one side while you make the flowers.

2 Mix yellow and green clay together then roll out a thin coil for the stem. Bend the coil into shape and place it on a piece of foil. Press some clay flat then, using a sharp craft knife cut out two leaves and arrange either side of the stem.

3 Blend white and blue clay. Roll out three balls of slightly different sizes. Flatten into thin circles, carefully fold one side over, then the other to form a bell shape. Press the largest onto the end of the stem then arrange the remaining two shapes. Follow the manufacturer's instructions and bake. When cooled, glue them onto the card.

Cute Cookie

We modelled a runaway gingerbread man from clay and popped him on this tasty-looking card! He's so easy to make – especially if you use a cookie cutter!

TIME: One-Two hours, plus drying time
DESIGNER: Kirsty Prescott

Top Tip
Acrylic paints dry quickly and have a shiny finish which does not need to be varnished.

1 Crease and fold a white card blank, 10.5cm x 14.5cm, and attach pale pink card to the inside back. Cut pink and white gingham paper to 8cm x 12cm and stick centrally to the front.

2 Roll out a 8cm x 10cm piece of clay to 3mm thick. Cut a gingerbread man with a sharp craft knife or cookie cutter. Leave to dry completely, or bake following the manufacturer's instructions. Then paint brown using acrylic paints.

3 Paint two black eyes and a mouth, two red buttons and white cuffs at the wrists and ankles. Wrap a thin cream ribbon around the neck and tie at the front in a small bow. Alternatively, stick on a pre-tied bow. Securely glue the gingerbread man centrally to the front of the card.

1   Flatten some clay with a rolling pin, or use your fingers for a more textured effect. Draw the outline of your cottage onto thin card and cut around it. Place this template onto your clay over a cutting mat, and carefully cut around the shape using a sharp craft knife.

2   Trim two strips of clay for the roof and press in place. Cut two clay squares for the windows and draw lines in a cross for the panes. Cut a door, a heart shape and three strips for the doorstep and windowsills. Place them all on the house.

3   Flatten three balls of clay for the smoke coming out of the chimney. Leave your cottage to dry then paint it with acrylic paints, add glitter and glue it onto the front of a card blank.

Top Tip
When joining two pieces of clay, always dampen both surfaces. If any parts fall off when dry, stick back on with some PVA glue.

Home Fires

This gorgeous moulded winter cottage makes a wonderful decoration for a greeting – and a perfect 'new home' card for someone who's on the move.

TIME: One hour, plus drying time
DESIGNER: Jill Alblas

Flower Power

Decorate this gorgeous jazzy card using flowers made from layers of soft candy-coloured clay mounted on bright pink card.

TIME: Two hours, with drying/baking
DESIGNER: Ellen Kharade

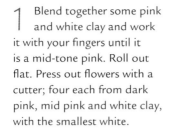

Top Tip
Batches of cards can be made really quickly using simple fondant cutters. Theme them to celebrate a special occasion.

1 Blend together some pink and white clay and work it with your fingers until it is a mid-tone pink. Roll out flat. Press out flowers with a cutter; four each from dark pink, mid pink and white clay, with the smallest white.

2 Place a dark pink, mid pink and white flower over each other. Gently push a pencil into the centre to stick them together. Make four flowers and bake in the oven.

3 Using a craft knife over a cutting mat, cut pale pink card, 22cm x 16cm, score and fold in half. Trim pink lustre paper, 7cm x 14.5cm, then a pink strip, 2cm x 11cm.

4 Place double-sided tape onto the back of the lustre paper and mount centrally onto the front of the card. Fix the pink strip in place. Cut a small length of pink braid and dab with a few spots of PVA, then attach. Glue the cooled flowers onto the card, equal distance apart.

1 From pretty motifs to decorated panels, polymer clay is such a versatile medium. For an individual look, stamp repeat patterns into the surface or add contrasting colours. Look around the house for interesting objects to make great imprints.

2 Trim white card, 21cm x 15cm and fold in half to make a blank. Mix white clay with a small amount of raspberry and blend until a pink marbled effect is achieved. Roll out thinly and trim into a 7cm square. Use a small heart-shaped cutter to gently press in nine motifs. Blend the marbled pink shade, in red to make a coral colour.

3 Roll out thinly and create nine smaller heart shapes with a cookie cutter. Press firmly into the centre of the larger ones. Finish by imprinting a flower design in between the motifs and oven bake. Glue the tile to the folded card to finish.

Bright Ideas

You're sure to have some fun objects around the house you can use to make impressions in polymer clay, like the heart cutter or daisy stamp used on this design.

Top Tip

Always follow the manufacturer's instructions carefully when baking polymer clay. If the oven temperature is too high or the clay is baked for too long it can become discoloured.

TIME: Two hours
DESIGNER: Jill Alblas

From the Heart

A pretty wire-and-bead detail transforms this simple clay heart into a token of love. It's easy to make for someone special and can be matched to any colour scheme.

TIME: 15 minutes, plus drying
DESIGNER: Jill Albas

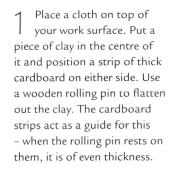

Top Tip
Never attempt to dry polymer clay quickly with direct heat, as this will make it warp and crack.

1 Place a cloth on top of your work surface. Put a piece of clay in the centre of it and position a strip of thick cardboard on either side. Use a wooden rolling pin to flatten out the clay. The cardboard strips act as a guide for this – when the rolling pin rests on them, it is of even thickness.

2 Cut a heart template from thin card, place it on the clay and cut around it with a craft knife. Use a thick needle to push a hole through the centre. Paint when thoroughly dry.

3 Cut purple card 16cm x 12cm, then fold in half. Glue white corrugated card, 9cm x 8cm, onto the front. Cut wire 25cm long and thread through the hole, then bend carefully so it lies flat on the back of the heart.

4 Wind the ends of the wire around a pencil to coil. Thread with a bead on the tip and fix with a dot of glue. Glue the heart to the centre of the white card.

1 Trim green plaid paper the length of a red card blank and half its width. Stick down the left side of the blank with double-sided tape. Punch out four large squares from white card and layer with green card. Stick to the blank with foam pads.

2 Punch two Christmas trees from green clay and stick to two of the squares with 3D foam. Decorate the trees with small yellow clay dots and stars. Make three pudding circles, two from brown clay and one from white.

3 Cut the white circles in half and stick to the brown ones with PVA glue. Punch out holly and berries, add to each pudding, and stick it to the card with foam pads. Stick a red clay dot in every corner of the squares.

Top Tip
These motifs will also make wonderful tree decorations – simply pierce a hole through before drying and thread with metallic twine for hanging.

Merry Makes

Festive cards are fun to make at any time of the year – especially when they're as gorgeous as this bright design decorated with polymer clay Christmas puddings and trees.

TIME: Two hours, with drying time
DESIGNER: Wendy Horrod

Electric Blue

Everyone loves to receive a show-stopping card like this one decorated with a tiny dovecote made from vivid pink and blue clay. It even has a white dove on the roof!

Top Tip
For modelling fine detail, nothing beats using a cocktail stick – they're cheap, reusable and widely available.

TIME: Two hours
DESIGNER: Corinne Bradd

1 Mould a rectangle from streaky pink clay and smooth until the back is flat and the front is rounded. Mark a series of regular indentations for the planks with a plastic ruler. Cut an arched window in the centre and add another strip of clay for the windowsill.

2 Cut tiny tiles from streaky blue clay and layer them onto the dovecote roof. Shape a tiny dove from white clay to go on the roof. Bake your dovecote in the oven. When cool, use gel pens to add further detail.

3 Trim a white card rectangle and mount onto pink card, leaving a 2mm border. Stick this panel to the front of an A5 blue card blank. Fix the dovecote to the centre with strong glue.

Happy Snaps

Turn treasured images into delightful mementos to send to friends and family

Photographs are a wonderful way to preserve important moments in life, whether they are ground-breaking events, or just heart-warming and amusing occasions. All too often however, these snaps wind up stuffed in boxes and forgotten. Albums are one option, but photographs can also be incorporated into greetings to create a card that is also a gift in itself.

Fond Memories

This project has a charming rustic feel, using warm shades of red, orange and brown. The design enables the photograph to be displayed on a mantlepiece or table, supported firmly by the flaps on either side.

1 Lay the red cardstock in front of you, with the long side horizontal. Score lines 5cm from each side lengthways, using a ruler and a bone folder to get a neat result. Crease the scored lines to create card front flaps.

You will need

Red, mocha, watermelon pink and light yellow card

Square patterned paper in blue and brown shades and pale blue paper

Daisy punch or die cut

Olive and light pink pastel chalk ink

Yellow organza ribbon, 56cm

Gold mini brad

Photograph

TIME: 45 minutes

PROJECT DESIGNER: Karen Weiderhold

2 Measure 6cm down each fold from the top and cut 1cm slots. These are to feed the ribbon through later. Glue the patterned paper inside the card on the back panel.

3 Colour the edges of the front flaps with light pink chalk ink. Trim the yellow cardstock to 6cm square and colour the edges with olive green chalk ink. Turn the square over and find its centre point by lightly drawing two intersecting pencil lines. Pierce this point with a small hole.

6 Thread the organza ribbon through the slots at both sides of the greeting, and fix to the patterned paper to secure it. Trim the ends of the ribbon to prevent fraying. Mount your chosen photograph on yellow cardstock and trim to leave a border all round.

Top Tip
This greeting is a great way to display a special photo, perhaps a wedding picture for family overseas who were unable to attend, or an anniversary portrait.

4 Die-cut or punch flower shapes from the brown cardstock and the blue patterned paper. Assemble and attach to the yellow section with a mini gold brad. Glue this down onto the watermelon pink cardstock, cut to 7.5cm square.

7 Stick the mounted photograph to the inside back panel of the card. Close the greeting and tie the ribbon in a bow at the front to fasten shut.

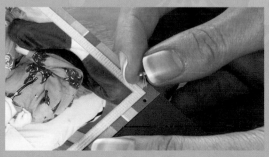

5 Stick the flower, yellow and watermelon layers down onto the mocha card, cut to 8.8cm square. Lightly glue down the petals to prevent them snagging on the ribbon. Apply adhesive to the back of this decoration down the left side only, and attach it centrally to the left front flap of the red card.

8 The card can be turned into a mini album or brag book by fixing two brads on the back panel on the left side, and then adding pages, 10cm x 15cm, to fit over the backing photograph. The brads allow pages to be added or removed.

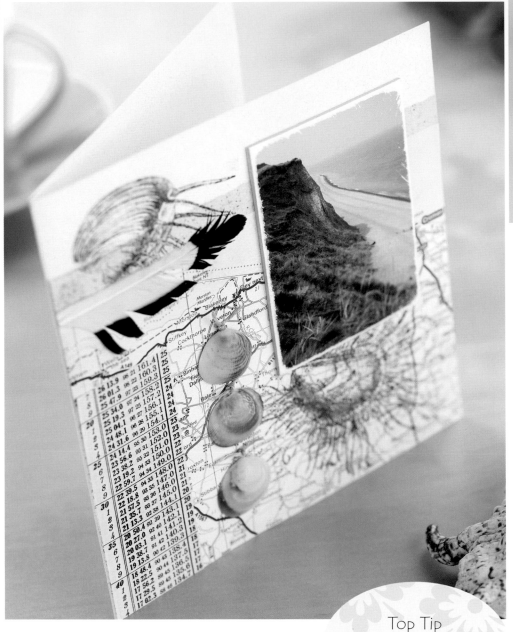

On the Tide

You can combine found items such as seashells and feathers with photographs to make unusual cards which have masses of texture and depth.

Top Tip
Do not allow the photocopy to move when transferring, or the image will be blurred.

TIME: 40 minutes
DESIGNER: Sarah Beaman

1 Trim a white fleck card blank, 14.5cm square. Snip handmade paper, 12cm x 14.5cm and glue on the blank. Cut map paper, 11cm x 14.5cm and stick. Trim latitudes/tide table paper, 8cm x 3.5cm and stick to the lower left corner.

2 Cut around a black and white photocopy of a shell, leaving a border. Dip a cotton bud into cellulose thinner and lightly wipe over the back. Position face down near the top left corner. Firmly rub with the back of a teaspoon, then remove to reveal the transfer. Repeat with a second shell photocopy, in the lower right corner.

3 Stick a photograph onto a mount. Trim to 8cm x 6cm. Distress the edges with an emery board. Fix near the top right corner. Attach three shells with a needle and waxy blue flax. Glue a feather in the top left corner and trim in line with the left edge.

Love Birds

Make a stylish wedding or engagement card in minutes using themed paper in muted tones and a simple stamped tag. It's an ideal last-minute make for a special occasion.

TIME: 25 minutes
DESIGNER: Caroline Blanchard

Top Tip
It's easy to change the theme of this card by using different torn paper and another stamped image on the tag.

1 Stick a layer of rich red card to silver mirror card and trim to leave a narrow silver border all round. Mount onto a slightly larger cream square card blank. Cut heart-patterned paper the width of the red card, tear off a strip and stick across the centre of the red card.

2 In black ink, draw or stamp a love bird or dove design onto cream card. Any romantic image would be suitable if you prefer an alternative to birds. Cut into a tag shape, layer onto red card and trim to leave a narrow border all round.

3 Add four small beads onto two earring wires. Stick these to the reverse of the tag, then attach it to the greeting using sticky foam pads. Attach a small silver peg to the top of the tag.

Funky Diva

Perfect for modern girls, this retro design made from eyecatching dotted paper and a simple stamped image is sure to impress the most discerning recipient!

Top Tip

If you stand up to apply pressure on a rubber stamp it is easier to achieve a more accurately placed image and an even finish.

1 Cut out a square of dotted paper slightly smaller than a cream square card blank. Stick to the front of the blank, keeping the fold at the top. Cut a smaller rectangle from black card.

2 Make a knot in a strip of ribbon, and fix it across the black card near the bottom edge, using double-sided tape and keeping the knot to one side. Attach the card in the centre of the dotted paper on the blank. Stamp a funky diva image onto white paper and trim.

3 Cut some light blue card the same size as the stamped white rectangle, and stick both pieces on the black panel at a jaunty angle to each other. To finish off your card, place a jelly label on the black card, running up the side of the stamped image.

TIME: 20 minutes

DESIGNER: Paula Whittaker

Water Baby

Card and paper in cool shades of blue and sizzling stripes make the perfect background for a precious baby photo – and a wonderful memento grandparents will love.

Top Tip

Gift wrap makes an inexpensive alternative to scrapbooking paper, and often provides just the pattern you need!

TIME: 20 minutes
DESIGNER: Jane Kharade

1 Fold white card, 13cm x 29cm, in half. Stick a turquoise rectangle, 12cm x 9cm, centrally to it and a smaller piece of purple paper on top. Add a panel of striped paper with the stripes running vertically.

2 Cut a photograph to measure 7cm x 4.5cm, and trim it with decorative-edged scissors across the top and bottom to create interest. Fix onto the striped paper. Blend turquoise polymer clay with white to make a paler shade of blue clay.

3 With a flower-shaped cutter, make five clay daisies. Bake in the oven and add a cabochon gem to each one with glue dots when cool. Fix to the card and add your own personal message.

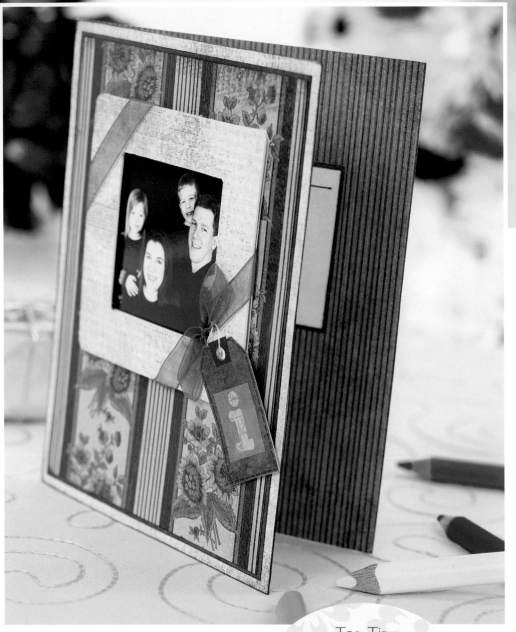

1 Cut and fold a 16.5cm x 25.5cm card blank. Cut the same size of textured, ivory paper, ink the edges black and attach to the blank. Cut 11.7cm x 15.5cm of blue flower patterned paper, apply black felt tip to the edges, stick to navy paper and trim, leaving a 2mm border. Attach to the blank. Cover a jumbo slide mount with more ivory paper.

2 Fix a photo behind the frame. Wrap sheer ribbon around the top left and bottom right corners, tying a bow on the front and stick down. Adhere the frame to the greeting. Take a navy tag, punch or pierce a 2mm hole at the top, and thread with string or a lace.

3 Snip a scrapbooking overlay alphabet tile and stick to the tag, using vellum glue dots. Fix the tag to the frame using sticky foam pads. Decorate the inside with 'welcome home' phrases from a definitions and words embellishment pack.

Home Coming

This photo greeting makes a wonderful welcome home card for family or friends. The photo is framed behind a decorated slide mount.

Top Tip
When using dark coloured card, write your greeting in gel or metallic pens that co-ordinate with the overall colour scheme.

TIME: 30 minutes

DESIGNER: Shauna Berglund-Immel

Retro Revival

Choose a bright funky ribbon and you have the starting point for a gorgeous photo memory card finished off with co-ordinating brads and mesh.

Top Tip
Using ribbon is a great way to enhance even the simplest card design. It's inexpensive and a small amount goes a long way.

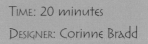

TIME: 20 minutes
DESIGNER: Corinne Bradd

1 Fold an A6 cream marbled card blank and fix two different size strips of co-ordinating magic mesh down each side, with the wider one on the right. Glue patterned ribbon down the left-hand side, close to the fold, and trim the ends.

2 Choose a small square black and white photo, and mount onto bright card in one of the ribbon colours. Print out a postage stamp-sized copy of the same picture and run around the edges in matching felt pen.

3 Mount both panels on the card lining them up with the mesh, and add a row of small metallic brads in the space between and below them. Place a large decorative brad in the top left corner of the main photo.

top dog

cat
collar
tassel

1 Make a 14.5cm square card blank. Trim aqua paper with brown spots, 14.5cm x 6cm, and stick the panel to the right edge of the card. Choose and print out a photo of your dog, trim to 11cm x 9cm, and adhere to the top left corner of the blank with spray glue.

2 Fix a length of continuous glue line from top to bottom of the greeting where the photo and paper meet. Position a length of narrow brown gingham ribbon on top of the glue.

3 Punch an aqua card circle, shade the edge with an ink-pad or felt-tip pen and stamp with a paw print. Pierce a small hole and thread the tag onto blue waxy flax. Tie to a dog bone clip and slide onto the top edge of the card.

Pet Shop Boys

Take a snap of a faithful companion and use your card making skills to turn it into a gorgeous greeting using an attractive brown polka-dot paper.

Top Tip
Using printed digital images means you will always have a spare copy if you give a photo away on a card!

TIME: 15 minutes

DESIGNER: Sarah Beaman

Cute Kitty

Delight a cat-lover with a special handmade greeting featuring their very own furry feline friend. What a wonderful way to suprise them!

Top Tip
If you don't have an alphabet stamp, try using transfer letters or stencil and ink as an alternative.

TIME: 15 minutes
DESIGNER: Sarah Beaman

1 Make a 14.5cm pink square card blank. Trim brown paper with pink spots, 14.5cm x 6cm, and stick to the right edge of the card. Print out a photo of your cat, trim to 11cm x 9cm, and adhere to the top left corner with spray glue.

2 Fix a length of continuous glue line from top to bottom of the greeting where the photo and paper meet. Lay a 15cm length of pink waxy flax across the adhesive, 16cm up from the base of the card, then position a length of gingham ribbon on top.

3 Punch a pink card circle, colour the edge with an ink-pad or a felt-tip pen and stamp on a paw print. Make a small hole and thread the tag onto the waxy flax.

Perfect Penwork

Shade your greeting with careful applications of colour, then outline in ink for a striking result

Pen and wash is a relatively simple technique to master, allowing you to create lovely cards. All it requires is a steady hand and a little care with the paintbrush and pen, ensuring each section you colour is completely dry before moving to the next. As you gain confidence, you might even wish to draw your own designs to paint.

Bear Necessities

This cute design would appeal to any child, or an adult fan of teddies! The suitcases would make this a perfect 'Bon Voyage' greeting to give to someone off on their travels.

You will need

Two plain card blanks

Two sheets of water-colour paper
11.5cm x 9cm

Tracing paper and transfer paper

Black waterproof fine liner pens, 05 and 02

Small clear plastic ruler, metal ruler

Eraser

Low tack masking tape and double-sided tape

Hairdryer

Stylus

A flat no. 6 paintbrush and
a round no. 2 paintbrush

Bubble palette

Kitchen roll

Water-colour paints: blue, pink, cream,
pistachio green, periwinkle blue

Craft knife and cutting mat

TIME: 30 minutes

PROJECT DESIGNER: Ruth Watkins

1 Cut one card blank in half down the fold. Trace the design from the template with the 05 fine liner pen. Centre the tracing onto one of the halves, securing with masking tape. Slip transfer paper underneath. Lightly go over the outlines using a stylus, and a ruler for all the straight ones.

2 When complete, remove the papers, easing the tape off gently. Lighten any heavy lines with an eraser, then go over them with the 05 pen, held fairly upright and not pressing hard. Set the ink with a hairdryer on the highest temperature, held close for one to two minutes.

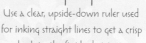

Top Tip
Use a clear, upside-down ruler used for inking straight lines to get a crisp look to the finished picture.

3 Mix one drop of pink paint with four drops of clean water. Dip the round brush into the wash and lightly touch the bristles on kitchen roll to remove excess. Colour the ears, around the nose, T-shirt, paws, straps and corners of top suitcase, tag and handle of bottom suitcase.

4 Make up washes of other colours as before. Dry adjacent sections to prevent bleeding. Paint floor, bear, tag and handle on top suitcase, then the fasteners and label of bottom suitcase with cream. Colour postcard and bottom suitcase periwinkle, and pistachio for top suitcase and stickers on the bottom one.

5 Dampen the background with a flat brush and apply blue wash. Build up the colours with further washes. Dampen shaded areas, pick up a little undiluted colour and blend, moving bristles back and forth. If you have too much paint or water, gently blot with kitchen roll and start again.

6 When all painting is complete, set with the hairdryer, then touch up the lines with 02 fine liner pen. Use the flat brush and undiluted pistachio to paint both sides of the small blank, and undiluted cream to the front of the remaining water-colour paper. Set with the hairdryer.

7 Trim around the teddy design card with the knife and metal ruler. Cut yellow card a little larger and stick the painted panel on top with double-sided tape, leaving a small border.

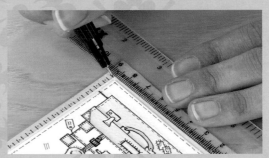

8 Stick to the front of the pistachio blank, leaving a slightly larger border at the bottom. Add stitching, dots and detail to finish with the 02 fine liner pen and ruler, using the picture as a guide. Add initials of your choice to the nameplate on the bottom suitcase.

Blossom Beauty

Every girl loves to receive flowers, so make this card and brighten someone's day. Hot pink and orange blossoms and sequins shimmer against the dark background.

1 Fold the white medium-weight card, 21cm x 15cm, in half. Then cut out a rectangle of black card or paper, 6cm x 15cm, and stick it centrally to the blank, leaving a white margin on either side.

2 Mix pink and orange ink and use to lightly colour some textured paper to give a variegated effect. Leave to dry. Cut out three blossom or flower shapes.

3 Use sticky foam pads to attach the flowers asymmetrically and to give a raised effect to the flowers. Complete by brushing the blossoms with a selection of pink, orange and red glitter, and add faceted pink sequins or gemstones to make flower centres. Decorate further by dotting a few sequins around the card, but don't overdo it.

Top Tip

This pretty and versatile card can be created in no time and is a great starter project for a beginner.

TIME: 15 minutes
DESIGNER: Jane Kharade

Flutter By

Use the wax 'n' wash technique to create beautiful butterflies. They're perfect for summer birthdays or as party invitations for social butterflies everywhere.

TIME: 15 minutes
DESIGNER: Jane Kharade

Top Tip

An easy one for children to help with – they will love to watch their images magically appear in front of them.

1 Fold white deckle-edged paper in two, leaving the raw edges. Use a pencil to lightly draw in the shape of a butterfly. With a white wax crayon go over the outline of the butterfly, pressing down quite heavily.

2 When thinking about which colours to use for your card, remember that darker, bolder colours work best as they look more striking, although lighter shades can be used alongside them to create contrast.

3 Slightly dampen the paper with a little water, apply lime green and yellow ink over the card and leave to dry. Finish off by adding glitter and gluing on an array of shimmering sequins in shades of green. This will make your card really stand out.

1 Trace the design from the templates on page 253, omitting detail, onto water-colour paper. Go over the lines with a waterproof black pen. Set the ink with a hairdryer and when the ink is dry, erase any pencil marks that you can see.

2 In a bubble palette, make up washes of paint in yellow, light blue, cinnamon and red colours. Use a round brush to colour in the different elements, referring to the picture as a colour and placement guide.

3 Set well with a hairdryer, then add the stitching detail with a fine pen. Trim into a blunted point (similar to the shape of the roof of a house) and mount onto a piece of pink card, then a larger cream blank. Ink the detail on both pieces using fine black pen.

Warm Welcome

Make an inviting greeting to welcome someone into their new home. This pen and ink drawing of a bird-house is sure to inspire them to nest in style.

Top Tip
Feel free to alter the colour scheme, but keep to the same number of colours – too many will complicate this simple card.

TIME: 30 minutes
DESIGNER: Ruth Watkins

Family Tree

This charming bird-house design will delight nature lovers and gardeners alike! Make it to welcome in a new season, after you hear the sounds of the first cuckoo.

Top Tip

Don't worry if your water-colour wash is not perfect – little imperfections add charm and individuality to your greeting!

TIME: 15 minutes
DESIGNER: Ruth Watkins

1 Trace the three bird houses design from the templates on page 253 onto a small piece of water-colour paper, omitting fine detail and stitching. Outline the design with a black waterproof pen. Set ink with a hairdryer.

2 Gently rub out any pencil marks that you can see. Then wet the background and brush with a wash of yellow paint. Coat the branch in a light brown colour.

3 Paint in the rest of the design with washes of yellow, green, blue and red, using the picture as a guide. Make sure that the paint and card have dried well before adding the details and stitching with a black waterproof pen. Trim and mount onto fuchsia card. Use an extra mount if preferred.

1 Trace and transfer the design from the templates on page 253 onto water-colour paper and go over the lines with waterproof black pen. Ink in a free-hand border making the tree design appear as if on a cushion. Set the ink with a hairdryer and erase any pencil marks.

2 In a bubble palette, make up washes of yellow, green, cinnamon and wine colour. Use a round brush to fill in the leaves and hearts, following the picture as a general guide.

3 Coat the background in cinnamon and blend wine round the edges of the 'cushion' to make it appear soft. Paint the background with a light blue wash. Add detail, then trim and mount on folded fuchsia card.

Heart to Heart

Washes of delicate colour make a subtle and understated greeting that's sure to impress. This hearts and tree design on a cushion is sure to brighten up a loved one's day.

Top Tip
Avoid heartache by keeping a roll of kitchen paper on hand to blot and mop up errors instantly.

TIME: 15 minutes
DESIGNER: Ruth Watkins

Oh Crumbs!

Paint up a sweet and sugary teatime treat without all the naughty calories! Give someone a sweet taste with this delicious cookie card that looks good enough to eat.

Top Tip

Make matching gift tags by tracing one element of the pattern (e.g. the cookie jar) and colour-washing it the same.

TIME: 30 minutes
DESIGNER: Ruth Watkins

1 Trace and transfer the cookie jar design from the templates on page 253 onto a small piece of water-colour paper, omitting the finer detail and stitching. Carefully draw over the outline with a black waterproof pen. Set with a hairdryer.

2 Gently rub out any pencil marks that you can see. Wet the background, then brush with a wash of cinnamon paint. Add a further layer to outline the main elements of the design, such as the plate and the cookie jar.

3 Paint in the rest of the design with washes of yellow, green, wine and light blue, using the picture as a guide. Dry well before adding details. To finish, trim and mount on folded lilac card.

1 Trace the snowman design from the template on page 253 onto water-colour paper. Lightly outline the design with a black waterproof pen and set with a hairdryer, then rub out any pencil marks.

2 Wet the background and brush with a wash of light blue paint, leaving the snow white. Colour the hat and scarf with orange and blue/green. Fill in the snowman's nose and cheeks with a watery cherry red.

3 Dampen the surface of the card then, in places, carefully float full strength green ink on the scarf area and light blue on the snowman and ground, to give a rich shaded effect. Trim and mount the design on a turquoise blank. Use a silver pen to write your greeting.

Winter Warmer

Our little snowman won't catch a chill with his snuggly scarf and hat. He's the perfect messenger to send warm wishes to a friend this Christmas.

Top Tip
If you don't want to draw an image yourself, choose a rubber stamp and remember to use a waterproof ink pad.

TIME: 30 minutes
DESIGNER: Ruth Watkins

Coffee Time

Make an adorable coffee morning card featuring a tall stack of chunky mugs. Use it to invite your friends round for coffee – or tea – and a chat!

Top Tip

Instead of a clean cut border – try using a perforator tool to cut a lovely 'postage stamp' edge, and omit the outer stitching.

TIME: 30 minutes
DESIGNER: Ruth Watkins

1 Trace and transfer the tea cup design from the template on page 253 onto a small rectangular piece of water-colour paper. Go over the lines in black waterproof pen. Set with a hairdryer and erase the pencil marks.

2 In a bubble palette, make up washes of paint in yellow, green, cinnamon, blue and wine. Paint the top cup green with a wine lip and the bottom cup blue with a wine lip and saucer. The background should be wine and the border should be cinammon.

3 Blend extra layers in areas to add shading and depth, such as the sides of the tea cups. Dry, then add stitching details. To finish, trim and mount onto a small fuchsia card.

Sewn Up

Sewing isn't just for clothes, it can also be used to create fabulously decorated greetings

Sewing might seem an odd way to create a card at first, but by using simple stitching techniques and a carefully chosen selection of fabrics, you can make very beautiful and unique designs. There is also a huge variety of pretty ribbons and shaped buttons available that make wonderful sew-on embellishments to add the finishing touch.

Folk Art

This card mixes simple cotton prints with ribbons, trims and sequins, along with basic hand stitching using embroidery threads. The sewing is a simple running stitch, which adds to the charming naïve look of the greeting.

You will need

Floral, gingham and spotted fabrics

Vanishing pen

Cream card blank, 13.5cm square

Iron-on interfacing

Blue gingham ribbon

Pink ric-rac braid

Pink pom-pom trim

Pale blue, pink and pale pink embroidery thread

Pale blue iridescent sequins

Pink seed beads

Lilac flower-shaped button

Double-sided tape

Fabric glue

TIME: 30 minutes

PROJECT DESIGNER: Sally Southern

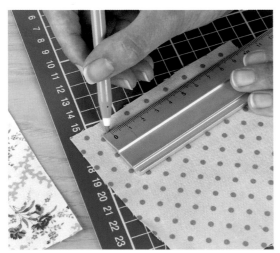

1 Take the spotted fabric and using a vanishing pen, mark out 8.5cm x 10cm. Draw another 10cm line, 3cm in from the left-hand edge. Back the floral fabric with interfacing by ironing it on.

2 Cut a strip of the bonded flowery material to go at the left-hand side of the spotted base fabric, so that it covers the first 3cm, up to the line drawn. Peel off the paper backing and press with the iron to fix in place.

3 Snip gingham ribbon and pink ric-rac braid, then glue, one on top of the other onto the spotted fabric, 1cm away from the floral strip. Turn the raw edges of the fabric panel under and press with the iron so that it measures 8.5cm x 10cm.

4 Pin, then add running
   stitch around the
edges using pale blue
thread. Sew a line of
running stitch in pink beside
the gingham ribbon. Make
small stitches attaching the ribbon to
the base fabric, also in pink.

Top Tip
Split the embroidery threads into
three strands. This makes it a little
thinner and easier to sew in such a
small area.

5 Sew sequins with pink seed beads in the centre, at the edge of the
   floral fabric. Trace flower and leaf shapes onto iron-on interfacing
and roughly cut out. This will stop the edges from fraying.

6 Iron the flowers and leaves onto
   the back of the appropriate
fabrics and trim. Peel off the paper
backing. Sew running stitch in pale
pink along the centres of the leaves.

7 Around the edge of the big gingham
   flower, sew running stitch in blue
thread. Place the smaller flower on top
and secure the two together by sewing a
button in the centre of the bloom.

8 Use double-sided
   tape to stick the
fabric square onto the
front of the card. Stick
the leaves and flowers in
place, then run a length of
pink pom-pom braid up
the left-hand side of the
card and secure on the
back with tape.

1 Fold A4 card in half to make a tall blank. Cut a centre panel with scallop edge scissors. Cut four, 4cm circles in different shades of card. Cut another four discs, 5cm in diameter.

2 Mark dots at even spaces around each circle and engrave with a stylus tool or an old ball-point pen. Use a 2mm circle hand punch or a tapestry needle to make holes at the marked points. Sew each in embroidery threads, using buttonhole stitch.

3 Stick the small circles onto the larger ones, pairing contrasting colours together. Punch or cut a flower and two star shapes in different colours. Cut a small heart shape. Add four 'buttonholes' to each one and fix in place on the circles. Pierce the holes through the card with a tapestry needle and stitch a cross on each. Fix each circle on top of each other in a line on the scalloped card.

Top Tip
Choose textured card for a more fabric-like finish. You can also try sewing on real buttons to decorate your card.

Stitch in Time
Combine thread and paper for cards that are easy to make, but look so special. The different shapes and textures create movement on this truly modern card.

TIME: One hour
DESIGNER: Susan Niner Janes

Strawberry Fields

Sweet, juicy, and bursting with flavour, this strawberry greeting is a summertime treat, and with its padded fruit and seeds made from beads, it looks good enough to eat!

Top Tip

To save yourself some time, use a white, pearly highlighter pen suitable for fabric instead of the beads and sequins.

TIME: One hour
DESIGNER: Kirsty Prescott

1 Cut two strawberry shapes from red felt. On one, sew sequins and beads at intervals, by bringing a needle and thread from the back to the front, loading a sequin then bead onto the needle, then taking the thread back through the middle of the sequin and felt to the reverse of the fruit.

2 Sew both pieces together around the edge using running stitch and red thread. Leave an opening, fill the strawberry with wadding, and tack closed. Cut two stalk shapes from green felt, fill with wadding and stitch using green thread.

3 Stick the stalk onto the strawberry, then fix the motif onto the centre of a white folded card blank, 14.5cm square, when folded.

First Steps

Team soft fabrics with jaunty striped vellum to make this welcoming card for a baby. By using two different techniques this multi-layered card is lots of fun to create.

Top Tip
Make this greeting for a girl with pink card, striped vellum and felt, stitched with blue thread for a nice contrast.

TIME: One hour

DESIGNER: Dorothy Wood

1 Cut a 2.8cm square from three different shades of blue felt. Draw a heart in the centre of one and a circle in each of the others. Using two strands of pink thread, work a row of back stitch along the line of the heart. Fill the centre with small stitches. Sew a row of lazy daisy stitches around the edge.

2 Work back stitch around the circles. Sew a flower in lazy daisy stitch in the centre of one and sew small straight stitches out from the circle. Work French knots around the second circle and finish with a star.

3 Cut 5.5cm x 13cm sections of stripe vellum and white paper. Tear the edges of the white paper. Trim bright blue card, 14cm square, score and fold in half. Glue the white paper on the blank. Position the vellum on top and stick the felt squares in place. Open the blank, punch 2mm holes in the corners of each square and insert eyelets to fix.

Wrapped Up

Give this card with a surprise gift, lovingly presented and finished with a bow. The blue ric-rac border creates a wavy effect and gives this birthday card a very special edge.

Top Tip
Choose textured card for a more fabric-like finish. You can also try sewing on real buttons as decorations.

TIME: One hour
DESIGNER: Kirsty Prescott

1 Cover a blank in blue spotted fabric using adhesive, smoothing any bubbles and creases out. Using the template on page 253, cut three presents from white felt. Glue these together to make one bulky present that stands out, and stitch around the edges in blue.

2 Stitch the ribbon detail in blue thread. Stick the felt present to the front of the card, placing it centrally. To decorate, iron on a few self-adhesive diamanté stones to the present and material, following the manufacturer's instructions carefully.

3 Stick ric-rac around the front of the greeting to make a pretty border. Then, following the edge of the ric-rac, cut the edges of the card for a wavy effect.

Sew Simple

Use small stitched detail to embellish this funky retro-look greeting; its contrasting colours, shapes and motifs make it 'sew' psychadelic – yeah, baby!

Top Tip

If time is an issue, only embroider a few flowers and use a fine ink pen to fill in the rest – the effect will be just as striking.

TIME: One hour
DESIGNER: Paula Pascual

1 Cut white card, 13.5cm square when folded in half. Trim pink and yellow paper, 12.5cm square, and colour the edges by holding the panel up and running a black ink-pad along the edges at a 90° angle. Position the paper on the front of the blank using double-sided tape.

2 Cut a circle of white card 10cm in diameter using a compass or cutting tool. Cut a 4cm hole out of the middle. For each embroidered flower, punch a set of holes using a fine needle. Here there are twelve holes around the outside and one in the middle for each flower. Make as many flower sets as you wish.

3 Embroider the flowers using black, yellow, pink and red thread. Colour the edges with a black ink-pad. Stick the embroidered ring in the centre of the blank with 3D sticky foam pads. Position a 'play' sticker in the middle of the ring.

Soft Centres

Stitch a stylish greeting, embellished with sparkling beads and sequins for a touch of romance. This funky modern heart will show your true love your true feelings.

TIME: One hour, 30 minutes
DESIGNER: Sally Southern

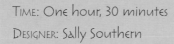

Top Tip
Cookie cutters make great templates to draw around for fabric or card. You can find some ideal shapes to use on your cards this way.

1 Trace a heart motif onto fabric. Decorate with strips of ribbon and other materials, running vertically. Use either fabric glue or bonding web to attach, and allow to dry if necessary.

2 Cut out and glue the edges with a clear glue so they won't fray. Decorate with stitching, beads and sequins. Stick onto the front of a purple blank.

3 Use a needle to prick holes around the design and sew seed beads directly onto the greeting. Finish by writing the words 'with love' and sealing it with a kiss along the bottom of the card.

Sew Cute

Get your favourite threads out to create a snazzy stitched card covered with growing flowers. It's ideal to send to a little girl who longs to be all grown up!

1 Cut a piece of lilac felt, 9cm x 12.5cm. Trace three flower shapes onto bonding web and roughly trim. Iron onto the back of floral fabrics and cut out to the required shape.

2 Carefully press a strip of bonding web onto a thin tape measure. Trim to give three stems and peel off all the backing. Arrange onto the felt and iron carefully, using a towel as a barrier between the card and iron.

3 Stitch the flowers and sew a button at the centre of each, using different coloured thread. Attach a selection of buttons along the bottom edge of the felt, choosing different shapes and sizes. Mount the completed panel onto the front of a cream card blank, using double-sided tape.

Top Tip
Take care not to melt the tape measures with the hot iron. Place fabric over when attaching bonding web, and also when ironing onto the card.

TIME: One hour
DESIGNER: Sally Southern

Fairy Wish

With her magic wand and sparkling wings, our smiling fairy will be a hit with the little girls. Her padded body and rosy cheeks magically bring this fairy to life.

Top Tip
By simply adding a halo you can transform this fairy design into a Christmas angel.

TIME: One hour
DESIGNER: Kirsty Prescott

1 Referring to the template on page 253, cut out two outline body shapes from white felt. Cut one peach felt face and one pale pink felt dress. Then one felt frill and two cheeks. Make the hair from yellow felt.

2 Sew all coloured pieces onto one of the white bodies using co-ordinating thread. Add white sequins to the wings and pink ones to the dress. Embroider black eyes, a red mouth and pink arms.

3 Place the decorated fairy body onto the plain one. Blanket stitch them together in white, leaving an opening. Stuff with toy filler or wadding and stitch to close. Attach the fairy to the front of a green blank using double-sided tape. Then cut a wand from gold card and stick down.

Beautiful Beading

Use bright, gem-like embellishments to give your greetings that extra sparkle

There are so many different types of beads available these days, from bright and funky to delicately coloured glass, and all kinds of shades and styles in-between. However, these are not just for jewellery; they can also be incorporated into the design of your cards either with stitching, wirework, or even just glue to really bring them to life.

You're A Star!

Capture soft and colourful mulberry papers between fine netting to create the perfect base for beading, sequins and delicate wirework. This lovely card would suit anyone with a taste for something a little different.

You will need

Purple card blank, 14cm square

Aqua card, 13cm torn square

Lilac folded insert

Pink and white mulberry paper

White fine net

Silver, pink and green embroidery threads

Needle

Turquoise wire

Round-nosed pliers

Assorted small sequins

Assorted small beads

Pink self-adhesive gems

Glue stick

Double-sided tape

TIME: 30 minutes

PROJECT DESIGNER: Glennis Gilruth

1 Tear a star from pink mulberry paper and fix it onto white mulberry paper with a light dab of glue in the centre. To get an accurate shape, paint around a star template with water to soften the mulberry paper, and then tear, holding the template in position as a guide.

2 Tear out the star again leaving a white margin around the edge and then place it between two squares of white net. Using round-nosed pliers, make two scrolls from 8cm lengths of turquoise wire. Stitch them both in the centre of the star, using tiny stitches in silver thread.

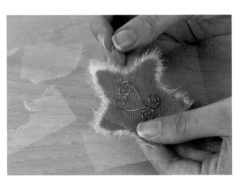

3 With the wire scrolls holding the paper and net layers together, pinch the net between your thumb and finger, and tear out the star, one layer of net at a time. If the net is difficult to tear, cut it with scissors and then distress the edges with tweezers.

4 Select seed beads, bugle beads, small gems and sequins in matching and contrasting colours. Using silver thread and tiny stitches, cover the surface of the star with embellishments. Avoid tangles by working with short lengths of thread and allow the thread to 'untwist' occasionally.

5 Take 24cm of turquoise craft wire and curl each end using the round-nosed pliers. Bend the wire in the centre and then twist the curls so that they each point in the same direction. Attach the wire to the reverse of the star with double-sided tape.

Top Tip
When working with beads and sequins, sprinkle a few onto a small tray and then replace all container lids immediately.

7 Take the aqua panel and, on the reverse, place strips of double-sided tape along two opposite edges. Working on one edge at a time, peel the protective layer to reveal the adhesive and press pink and green threads, in random loops, so that they are visible from the right side.

6 Tear a pink mulberry paper heart, attach it to a scrap of white mulberry paper and then tear it out again, leaving a narrow white margin. Place a small paper flower motif and a tiny sequin in the centre of the heart and stitch them into place using fine silver thread.

8 Attach the aqua panel to the purple card blank, using double-sided tape. Make a small hole in the top left corner of the card blank and add a twist of mixed threads. Affix the star and heart motifs using double-sided tape and then add a sprinkle of self-adhesive gems.

Gorgeous Garland

This card is great for using up those oddments of leftover seed beads. It will make a perfect Mother's Day card or simply send it to say 'thanks' to mum on any day of the year.

TIME: 30 minutes
DESIGNER: Gillian Slone

Top Tip

For this project, keep different types of beads in separate dishes while working, to make it easier to find the ones you want.

1 Using a size 12 needle and beading thread, string 13cm of green seed beads (size 11). Work back along beads, skipping the final one and threading the next two. Thread three gems. Ignoring the last, run through the other two to make a branch. Pass through the next two gems on the main stem.

2 Continue adding branches, varying the number of beads between. Randomly add flowers; string four pink seed beads and one yellow (size 11). Go back through the first pink in the opposite direction. Thread three pinks and pass through the fourth initially strung. Weave into the green beads.

3 Join the garland's stem ends. Cover half an 8cm x 20cm purple blank with patterned vellum. Secure ribbon over the join. Using glue, attach the garland to a 6.5cm circle of white card. Make small sprigs of bead 'flowers' and glue to tiny circles. Attach to card.

Super Stars

Beading is not always quick, but these stars are worth making the extra effort. The result is this heavenly card that will shine out from on top of the mantelpiece.

TIME: 30 minutes
DESIGNER: Gillian Slone

Top Tip
Substitute the bugle beads with two or three different coloured seed beads for a slightly varied look.

1 With a size 12 needle and beading thread, string five silver gems (size 11) together. Go back through to form a circle. Pick up a turquoise bead (size 11), run through the next silver of the circle. Repeat four times. Pass through first turquoise bead. String turquoise, silver, turquoise beads. Go through next turquoise of the previous round. Repeat four times.

2 Weave to emerge from a middle silver gem on the row just completed. String a silver bugle, turquoise and silver bead. Pass through just the turquoise the opposite way. Add a bugle. Run through the next middle silver gem. Repeat, making five points. Secure thread.

3 Make two more stars and a fourth reversing colours. Attach three to 3.5cm white scalloped squares. Fix to 11cm square turquoise card with foam pads. Glue fourth star onto card. Glue to a 14.5cm square white blank.

1 Using a sharp craft knife over a cutting mat, cut an aperture in a pearlescent blank, 4cm square, and back with green fabric using double-sided tape. Trace both flower shapes from the template on page 254 onto bonding web and iron onto fabric. Cut out both, then peel off the smaller flower's paper backing and place on the larger one. Iron to fix.

2 Peel off the larger flower's backing and stick onto the front of the card, overlapping the aperture. Press with the iron, layering it first with fabric to protect the card from scorching. Sew small running stitches around the edge in pink thread. Decorate with beads and sequins to finish. Use the sequins to make the flower petals glisten.

In the Frame

This pretty floral card will brighten up anyone's home, and everyone's day! Stitching and sequins will bring this flower to life so that it looks good enough to pick.

Top Tip
When sewing onto card, prick the holes first with a pin to make your stitches super neat.

TIME: 40 minutes
DESIGNER: Sally Southern

Golden Oldie

Mellow shades of autumn make a subtle backdrop for this exotic beauty. Gold on red and stunning glass beads make this bejewelled greeting fit for a queen.

TIME: 30 minutes
DESIGNER: Jill Alblas

Top Tip

Beaded cards can topple over, but a three-panelled version will give you extra stability; our beads rest slightly on the surface.

1 Take a piece of white card, 21cm x 14cm, then score and crease it to make three panels, each 7cm x 14cm. Glue red embossed paper onto the card. Press gently over the surface to ensure the paper is stuck down firmly and evenly onto the card.

2 String three, separate rows of gold and glass beads onto gold thread. Make sure each line does not exceed 6cm in length. Cut a piece of gold card, 5.5cm square, then carefully glue a smaller square of filigree paper onto it, close to the base of the card. Turn it over and tape the threaded beads onto the back so that they are more secure.

3 Fix four, double-sided sticky tabs onto the back of the gold card. Press it down on the front of the greeting. The best way to do this is to stand it upright first, so that you can make sure the gold card and beads are positioned correctly.

Tie The Knot

Make something a little different for a couple's big day with this oriental-style greeting. Beads sewn onto ribbon create these delicate bridal slippers with an exotic look.

Wedding Shoes

Top Tip
Assemble all the materials before starting, and try out different colour combinations by placing beads and ribbon together.

TIME: One hour

DESIGNER: Amanda Walker

1 Take wide gold satin ribbon and sew nine rocaille beads along one edge. Sew three gold sequins in a row and attach a rocaille in the centre of each. Fill the gaps in between with silver-lined glass beads. Tack bugle sparklers in a zigzag pattern. Stitch another row of rocailles to the other edge. Cut the beading from the ribbon, leaving 1cm either side. Repeat on another strip.

2 Draw and cut two simple sole shapes from Japanese paper (reverse one to make a pair). Stick double-sided tape to the undersides and fix the ribbon ends underneath. Cut a rectangle out of the patterned sheet and a slightly smaller one from glitter card.

3 Thread a narrow length of ribbon through a silver bell and tie in a bow. Add lettering onto separate paper using transfers or type. Assemble the greeting using spray glue for the shoes and a glue dot for the ribbon.

Patched Up

Use colours and textures, plus a little sewing and gluing, to create this eye-catching card. It makes a beautiful birthday card, or simply a cheery 'hello' to a special friend.

TIME: 30 minutes
DESIGNER: Glennis Gilruth

Top Tip
When sewing beads and sequins onto paper, use a perforator and, resting on the spongy side of an old mouse mat, make all the holes before stitching.

1 Cover the front of a white blank, 13cm square, with red textured card, wrapping it around the side fold and attaching it in place with double-sided tape. Trim the top, bottom and opening edge. Attach a piece of white perforated panel torn to 7.5cm x 7cm, in the centre of the card with tape.

2 Perforate and tear pink card, 2.5cm x 5cm, and pass it through a ribbler. Sew on three green bugle beads and a flower sequin. Make a turquoise card panel, 4cm x 4.5cm and decorate with a pink paper heart, beads and flower sequins. The turquoise panel will contrast well with the pink card.

3 Attach the decorated panels onto the white perforated section with double-sided tape. Make a tiny bow out of narrow yellow ribbon and fix to the blue square with a glue dot. Finish off by stitching a ribbon trim to the pink panel.

Retail Therapy

Miniature motifs are always intriguing and are so easy to make using tiny beads and sequins. As handbags are a girl's best friend, make this card for a fashion queen.

1 Using the template provided on page 254, cut a bag from pink card. Fold where indicated and sew a sequin and bead on the flap. Attach a string of orange seed beads to form the handle. Make a necklace with tiny green sequins and blue bugle beads.

2 Tear several small circles of yellow handmade paper, layer together and top with a self-adhesive red heart. Thread a needle with green and lilac sewing threads and pass it through small flower sequins and beads to form a mini-garland.

3 Attach the bag, necklace, heart motif and mini-garland in the centre of a turquoise card blank, using PVA. Tie a pink chiffon ribbon near the fold of the card to finish off.

Top Tip
For neatness and precision, use a cocktail stick when applying PVA adhesive to small motifs – they will be easier to handle.

TIME: 30 minutes
DESIGNER: Glennis Gilruth

Sugar and Spice

Make sure you'll always remember what your little girl is made of with this dainty greeting. Pretty in pink, this card is perfect for your little flower.

Top Tip

Two-toned paper will give striking results. If lacking confidence using a craft knife, try wrapping paper – its thin, slick surface makes cutting a lot easier.

TIME: 30 minutes

DESIGNER: Tracey Daykin-Jones

1 Make a 12cm square card blank from bubblegum pink card and fold in half. Cut a slightly smaller spotted panel to go on the front of the blank, and stick, leaving a thin border all around.

2 Trim a rectangle of bubblegum pink card and layer with a matching striped patterned paper, leaving a small border and rounding the bottom two corners for a retro look. Fix this panel to the centre of the greeting, positioning it closer to the top of the card, as shown.

3 To create the flower – the card centrepiece – glue six clear crystals vertically down the middle for the flower stem. Attach a flower posy button above it and some leaves below it using small strips of double-sided tape.

Lovely Lacé

Create complex-looking, yet easy to make
interlocking paper designs

The term lacé comes from a French word meaning
'linked together'. It began life as a selection of
products from a Dutch company, but quickly
evolved into a technique in its own right. Lacé
involves cutting from two-toned card, paper or
vellum using a metal template. The flaps are then
folded over and tucked under the piece in front,
revealing the contrasting colour or pattern.

Petal Power

This lovely greeting appears very intricate, but
is simple to create. The contrasting patterns
either side of the paper create a stunning
effect, complemented by pretty paper flowers.

You will need

Lacé template number 7

Lacé knife

Cutting mat

Two-toned wrapping paper

Low-tack, double-sided tape

Sticky-backed ribbon

Large and medium circle punches

Assorted pink buttons

Large and small white paper flowers

Large pink flower sequin

A4, pale pink and dark brown card

Glue

TIME: 15 minutes

PROJECT DESIGNER: Melanie Hendrick

Top Tip

Two-toned paper will give the most striking results. If lacking confidence using a craft knife, try wrapping paper – its thin, slick surface makes cutting easier.

1 Cut two-toned wrapping paper, 15cm square. Centre the lacé template onto the paper and secure with low tack tape. Start cutting left of the black reference dot on the template. Put the lacé blade into the template opening at a 90 degree angle.

2 Relax the knife in your hand as though you are holding a pen. If you hold on tightly, you will push down too hard which makes cutting difficult and causes the knife to dig into the mat, creating unnecessary drag.

3 Move the knife along the slot with pressure, then at the end of the opening, come up at a 90 degree angle. Use your arm movement to make the cut, always towards your body. Moving the knife away, sideways or changing the angle will cause inconsistencies in the slits.

4 Rotate the template as you cut to make it more comfortable. Cut all the openings in this way until you return to the black reference dot. Gently remove the template, being careful not to damage the paper.

5 Working anti-clockwise, fold the points over and tuck them under the smaller points to achieve the lacé effect. Take the A4 pink card, score and fold in half. Mount the finished lacé square onto the front of the blank, using double-sided tape.

6 Trim some more two-toned paper 6cm x 15cm. Stick at the bottom of the blank, with the alternate pattern to the lacé square uppermost. Snip a length of sticky-backed ribbon to the width of the blank, and cover the join between the contrasting papers.

7 Punch three medium circles, and a large one from dark brown card. Decorate the smaller punched circles with paper flowers, then stick a pink button to the centre of each one. Glue a large bloom to the larger circle, followed by a large flower sequin, then a pink button. Set all aside to dry.

8 Fix the three smaller shapes onto the lower patterned panel, using glue. Position them in a row, with the middle one near the top, and the other two close to the bottom. Attach the bigger punched flower circle in the middle of the lacé square.

1 Cover a thin, bright pink A6 card blank with hand-printed floral paper. Holding a sharp craft knife firmly but lightly, cut a curved lattice border strip, 1cm from the right-hand edge using a lacé template. Score the folds and interlace the design as shown.

2 Mount the lacé onto a paler pink A6 blank and trim the edges away neatly with a craft knife. Cut narrow strips of co-ordinating plain and hand-printed paper.

3 Glue the strips down the card on the left-hand side and the right-hand edge, placing them as shown in the photograph. To finish, decorate the lattice pattern with small round gemstones, held in place with PVA glue or glue dots.

In Bloom

Pinks, purples and floral patterns marry perfectly for a beautiful greeting and the watercolour-style handprinted paper makes the perfect backdrop to this stylish card.

Top Tip
Always hold the lacé knife vertically as you cut to get an even finish. Avoid having to cut the paper twice.

TIME: 20 minutes
DESIGNER: Corinne Bradd

Big Blossom

Create a huge floral design that will stand out proudly on any mantelpiece. The bright contrasting colours and shapes, and gemstone centre add to its contemporary feel.

Time: 20 minutes
Designer: Corinne Bradd

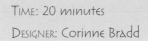

Top Tip

Only cut a line once, as going over it again will create a jagged edge; hold the knife upright as you cut for good precision.

1 Cut a large, half flower shape from orange and brown duo card using a lacé template and cutting knife. Fold every other section back to create a complete bloom and trim the strip of card at the spine to within 1mm of the folds.

2 Glue the flower to a square of bright pink vellum and use the template to cut the right-hand side into petals to match. Mount onto a rectangle of orange, pink and brown block patterned paper.

3 Mount the paper onto a large cream blank, ensuring there is an equal border of 2mm all the way round. To finish, stick a large pink gemstone to the centre of the flower using glue dots.

Bermuda Triangle

This simple lacé pattern creates a stunning effect when folded to reveal contrasting colours. This stylish card looks clever but is surprisingly simple to make.

1 Use a lacé template to cut a triangular lattice pattern from an oversize A6 piece of striped card with a coloured reverse side. Using a craft knife over a cutting mat, cut 2.5cm from the right-hand side. Score and fold the triangles down and interlock.

2 Score and fold the card 10.5cm wide and fix the back strip to the fold of a turquoise A6 blank, leaving the front piece loose. Trim the card at the top and bottom to neaten it up.

3 Cut thin strips of turquoise card and glue at random down the front of the card, using the photograph as a guide. Decorate each triangle point with a small turquoise mosaic sticker, taking care to make them all line up.

Top Tip
Push the knife into every corner and tilt to cut right to the end, pressing lightly but firmly; relax your hand as though holding a pen.

TIME: 20 minutes
DESIGNER: Corinne Bradd

Madame Butterfly

Cut and fold a colourful border for this lovely card and use pretty red butterflies as decorative motifs. It's ideal for celebrating an engagement or exam success.

Top Tip

When you have finished cutting, turn the template and paper over to check you have gone over all of the design before removing.

TIME: 20 minutes
DESIGNER: Corinne Bradd

1 Trim a piece of dark and light green duo card, 4cm x 15cm. Centre a lacé border template down the strip and cut out the design with a sharp craft knife, using an even pressure. Score and fold the points, interlocking each into the one below.

2 Glue the panel to the edge of a bright pink A6 blank, leaving a 2mm border at the edge. Cut three, 3cm squares out of the remaining card and back with a 4cm wide strip of duo card.

3 Decorate the left-hand edge of the design strip with a piece of thin pink satin ribbon, fastened on with double-sided tape. Fix three bright pink, padded satin butterflies in the centre of the squares with a dot of PVA, each positioned differently.

Border Patrol

It's hip to be square with this purple lacé greeting, embellished with dainty quilling in the centre and corners. Send it to a friend to let them know you're thinking of them.

1 Cut an 11cm square border pattern from purple card, using a lacé template. Start cutting left of the black reference dot on the template. Score and fold the design, then interlock the points.

2 Mount the pattern centrally onto a lilac pearlescent blank, 14.5cm square. Cut four, 5mm wide strips of co-ordinating striped card. Position them 3mm from the pattern to form a border, mitring the corners neatly by scoring and folding.

3 Make a simple quilled flower to stick in the centre of the design with three quilled green leaves. Create four quilled circles and glue them at each corner, positioned on the ribbon borders as shown.

Top Tip
Master the simple art of quilling by following the step-by-step instructions in the section on page 198.

TIME: 20 minutes
DESIGNER: Corinne Bradd

Just For You

Add a personal touch to this delightful lacé greeting, decorated with a tulip motif. Why not write a special message and conceal it in the tiny envelope attached to the card?

TIME: 45 minutes
DESIGNER: Jo Gratwick

Top Tip
Go over the corners with the knife to free the cut design before folding and creasing.

1 Secure a no. 37 lacé template to a strip of pearlescent pink paper (white on reverse) with low-tack tape, and cut the design. Remove the template carefully, checking that the cuts you have made meet, especially in the corners. Fold and crease alternate cut shapes, and tuck under the next design to finish the pattern.

2 Fold A4 card to form a blank and attach the lacé panel, 2cm from the top. Fix a pearlescent pink mini envelope in the bottom right corner. Trim 'Just for you' embossed card to fit, round the corners and punch a hole at the centre top.

3 Cut four lengths of dusty pink thread, 12cm long. Pull the middle of this bundle through the tag, pass the ends through the loop and trim. Attach using tape. Tie a double length of thread around the fold of the card and knot the ends to finish.

1 Cut A4 white or pink card, 12cm x 24cm, score and fold in half. Secure a no. 36 lacé template to dusty pink pearlescent paper (pale pink on reverse) with low tack tape and cut the design carefully using a sharp craft knife over a cutting mat.

2 Remove the template carefully, checking that the cuts you have made meet, especially in the corners of the design. Fold and crease alternate shapes, and tuck these under the next design to finish the pattern.

3 Attach the lacé design to A4 chocolate brown card and trim leaving a 5mm border all round. Secure the lacé to the centre of the card blank. To finish, place a peel-off greeting of your choice in the blank centre of the lacé design.

Compare and Contrast

Two-toned paper forms an intricate pattern that can't fail to impress. The spectacular array of colours arranged in a symmetrical garland shape makes a gorgeous greeting.

Top Tip
Sticky tabs can be used as an alternative to low tack tape – their handy holding strip can help if you find tape tricky to handle.

TIME: 45 minutes
DESIGNER: Jo Gratwick

In the Pink

This gorgeous lacé design is simple yet stunning, and can be adapted to any occasion. The pretty pattern and bright colours will brighten anyone's day.

Top Tip

Intricate lacé patterns are beautiful as the centrepiece for a greeting, and often don't need any extra decoration.

TIME: 45 minutes
DESIGNER: Jo Gratwick

1 Secure a no. 14 lacé template to dusty pink pearlescent duo card (white on reverse) with low-tack tape and cut the design with a lacé knife. Relax the knife in your hand as though you were holding a pen. Avoid gripping it too tightly and pushing down hard, because this will make cutting more difficult and cause the knife to dig into the mat.

2 Remove the template carefully, checking that all the cuts meet properly, especially in the corners. Fold and crease alternate shapes, and tuck these under the next design to finish the pattern.

3 Attach the design to the centre of a pearlescent white embossed blank, 12.5cm square, or a plain version the same size.

Dazzling Die-Cuts

Create perfect-looking shapes for your cards every time, without scissors or craft knives

Die-cutting is a simple, effective way for creating a multitude of paper motifs. This is done with a single machine, into which you put a 'die' with the design you want and punch it out. You can buy a huge variety of different dies, as well as the cutting tools, some of which can also be used for embossing.

Toy Story

This sweet baby card looks especially cute with a tiny teddy peeping out. The greeting uses three different types of die-cut, including a bear and tiny hearts to decorate the front, plus the small envelope.

2 Using a die-cutting machine and an envelope die, cut a petal envelope out of the gingham embellishment paper. Fold in the side flaps and turn up the bottom tab, gluing it in place. Leave the top flap unfolded.

Top Tip
Using a themed set of patterned papers, available in many styles and designs, will ensure that the end result is perfectly colour co-ordinated.

1 Cut the flowers embellishment paper to 13.5cm square and carefully glue to the front of the white card blank. Trim the plain pink embellishment paper to 11cm square and fix centrally over the flowers paper.

3 Attach the envelope to the card with sticky foam pads, sitting it on the left-hand side as shown. Punch three small hearts from white card and glue them in the lower right-hand corner of the pink square.

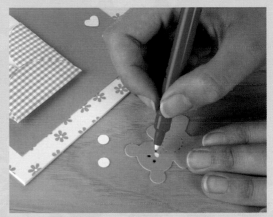

4 Use the die-cutting machine and a teddy bear die to create a shape in plain pink paper. Stick a small strip of white card on the reverse of the bear's head to cover the eye and nose holes. This will provide a base for adding his features.

5 Turn the teddy over to face you. Use a fine-tip black marker to draw in the face. Punch two small circles in white card using the single-hole punch and glue in place for the ears. Cut a larger oval and glue in place for the middle.

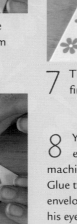

6 Slip the teddy into the envelope but leave his arms and head protruding. Fasten him in place with 3D sticky foam pads.

7 Tie a length of pink organza ribbon around the card, finishing with a bow positioned above the bear's head.

8 You can easily produce a matching envelope for this card. Use the die-cutting machine to cut out a teddy in gingham paper. Glue the bear in the top left-hand corner of the envelope, adding ears as before and drawing in his eyes, nose and mouth with the black pen. Punch three small hearts in pink paper and fix these in the lower right-hand corner.

In the Can

Make a green-fingered greeting that's perfect for gardeners. The muted tones of the textured papers reflect a garden and contrast well with the shiny silver of the watering can and tools.

Top Tip
Tear the textured paper using a ruler if you don't have ripple-edge scissors – the effect is just as nice.

TIME: 30 minutes
DESIGNER: Hayley Frost

1 Draw a watering can shape, and a trowel and a fork head on paper. Lay silver craft foil over your drawings and use masking tape to secure it in place. Place the sketch face up on a cutting mat and use a texture tool to trace the designs, pressing evenly and firmly.

2 Remove the drawn template and carefully cut the shapes, just outside the lines. Re-define the edges and add details such as rivets and sprinkler holes with the texture tool. Cut out brown paper, 15.5cm x 12.5cm, using ripple-edged scissors.

3 Trim a slightly smaller piece of mid-green textured paper, then a smaller piece of dark green card, 8cm x 10cm, layer the two together and stick them down. Snip two handles from brown paper and shade with a pen. Attach with double-sided tape to the dark green paper. Attach everything to a cream blank.

Clever Togs

Rustle up this cute ensemble to welcome a newborn tot into the world. Swap the blue background colour with the pink clothes depending on if it's a boy or a girl.

Top Tip
If you don't have a die-cutting machine, draw templates of these simple shapes, cut out and draw around.

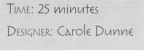

TIME: 25 minutes
DESIGNER: Carole Dunne

1 Begin with a white card blank, 8cm x 18cm. From a piece of blue card, cut a strip 4.5cm wide and stick across the bottom of the white blank. Place a white chain peel-off border along the top edge of the blue panel.

2 Using a baby clothes die set, make up the three garments from different shades of pink card. Attach 3D sticky foam pads onto the back of the shapes, then arrange them along the border line.

3 Punch two blue flowers and one white flower, and glue onto the card where they contrast with the card below. Add a little sparkle with silver peel-off dots placed in the centre of each floral shape. Stick on a silver greeting in the bottom left corner to finish.

Baby Steps

Create great motifs for card and paper with a speedy die-cutting system, then you'll be prepared with a card for those occasions when baby arrives early!

1 Take a white A5 folded card. Using a small and a medium circle punch, create a mixture of cream and soft green discs from sheets of coloured card. We used four medium cream discs, five small green discs and one large green and one small cream disc.

2 Glue these into place positioning some to the sides of the card and cutting off extras with a scalpel. From green, cut a 6.5cm square and attach to front. Trim a 5.5cm square from cream and place on top of the green square with 3D sticky foam pads.

3 Cut a romper suit or similar in green and glue on a collar and sash die-cut from white card. Finish by fixing a small green greeting near the base of the card.

TIME: 20 minutes
DESIGNER: Carole Dunn

It's Bliss

Make this beautifully simple card with bold colours and easy-to-use lettering. You can change the lettering to suit any occasion or sentiment you like.

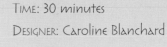

Top Tip

Tailor the sentiments on this greeting so that they are appropriate for any occasion.

TIME: 30 minutes

DESIGNER: Caroline Blanchard

1 Cut a piece of purple gingham paper to fit the front of a folded card blank and large enough to wrap around the fold. Carefully stick to the greeting using double-sided tape. Trim to size as necessary using a craft knife over a cutting mat.

2 Snip a rectangle of purple card, 4.5cm x 9.5cm, and stick down centrally onto the front of the decorated blank.

3 Cut out two orange flowers from card, using a die-cutter, hand tool or punch and stick them into position with double-sided tape or glue. Use rub-down lettering to add words, such as 'happy', 'delight' and 'bliss' to complete the card.

1 Create three different-sized heart motifs from two shades of card using a die-cutter, punches or freehand. Stick the hearts together with double-sided tape. Cut a square of mauve paper just bigger than the largest heart motif.

2 Using scallop edgers, cut out a slightly bigger square from textured paper. Stick the heart onto the first piece using 3D sticky foam pads. Fix to the second square using double-sided tape. Make the other two heart squares the same way.

3 Cut out an oblong of textured paper to match one of the colours used on the hearts. Mount the three heart squares onto the oblong, then fix onto the front of the card blank with double-sided tape.

Heart Throb

Why not wear your heart on your sleeve and treat the love of your life to a beautiful handmade card? Then they'll know for sure that you're their amour.

Top Tip
Cut one of the hearts from patterned paper to add an interesting twist to this layered card.

TIME: 30 minutes
DESIGNER: Hayley Frost

Big Love

Easy-score templates give bold designs a professional finish every time and the clever use of ribbon, weaved and in bows, will please the most hopeless of romantics.

Top Tip
Make this card without the eyelets by punching a hole through the middle of each heart with a hole punch.

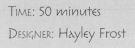

TIME: 50 minutes
DESIGNER: Hayley Frost

1 Cut out four heart shapes in graduating sizes, using a die-cutting machine or freehand, from two contrasting shades of paper. Place the motifs on top of one another, in alternate colours, then using eyelets and a setting tool, join them.

2 Tie a bow of sheer ribbon through the eyelets. Cut out a rectangle of cream paper using scallop paper edgers. Fix on the two heart arrangements with double-sided tape.

3 Cut a slightly larger rectangle of mauve paper. Stick together and mount onto a card blank using double-sided tape. Fix eyelets around the edge of the scalloped paper, through the card blank. Weave thin, mauve ribbon in and out. Tie with a bow.

Barrow Boy

Overflowing with tasty fresh vegetables, our card is just delicious – send it to the keen allotment holder or to celebrate Harvest time in the abundant summer months.

Top Tip

Use plain card instead of silver foil if you wish, adding edging detail with pen for a 3D effect.

TIME: 40 minutes
DESIGNER: Hayley Frost

1 Draw a wheelbarrow design on paper. Lay the sketch over silver craft foil and secure using masking tape. Place on a cutting mat and with a texture tool trace the shape, firmly and evenly.

2 Remove the drawn design and carefully cut the shape outside the textured line. Add details including rivets on the back of the foil. Draw and trim the vegetable outlines and the wheelbarrow handle, leg and wheel from coloured papers.

3 Use a star punch to make the tomato stalks. Cut out brown paper, 13.5cm x 10.5cm, using scallop-edged scissors and mount a smaller piece of green on top.

4 Position the elements and when happy, glue down starting at the back. Apply the barrow body with double-sided tape, making sure it lines up with the wheel and leg. Mount on a large card blank.

New Leaf

Make an eye-catching greeting with a seasonal theme. The bright oranges and yellow colours of the leaves will warm and delight as the nights are drawing in.

TIME: 30 minutes
DESIGNER: Peter Hughes

Top Tip
Use fresh green tones for springtime crafting, purples and yellows, too.

1 With a circle die or punches, cut out eight shapes, four large and four smaller from brown, orange and yellow card. Take a pale yellow or cream blank and cut away a 3cm strip from the right-hand edge. Make an insert from brown card, securing with glue at the spine.

2 Attach the smaller circles to the four large ones and fix along the front right-hand edge of the blank. Use a loopy border template and cut out from brown and orange card. Glue down each side.

3 Punch a hole in each circle and thread raffia through. Using two different die-cut leaves, cut a brown and orange craft foam shape from each. Select a worded rubber stamp of your choice and load it with brown ink.

4 Use a heat gun directly on an orange leaf. Stamp when the edges curl up. Use orange or yellow ink on the brown leaves and attach.

Elegant Embossing

Create beautiful raised designs with brightly coloured powders – just add heat

Raised embossing is such an easy technique, yet the results are stunning. First, an image or text is stamped onto paper, then, while the pigment is still wet, the entire motif is sprinkled with embossing powder, which is then heated. This activates the powder which melts, becoming raised and shiny as it dries, giving a three-dimensional effect.

Baby Steps

This simple yet effective greeting is perfect for welcoming a new arrival. The card is made using a subtle scrapbooking paper decorated with a stitched pattern, and the minimum of colours and embellishments.

You will need

Baby feet stamp

Double-sided blue patterned paper

Blue ric-rac

White and denim blue card

Blue button assortment

White narrow ribbon

Double-sided tape

Watermark ink pad

Diamond glaze glue

Silver embossing powder

Heat gun

TIME: 15 minutes

PROJECT DESIGNER: Tracey Daykin-Jones

1 Trim white card, 26cm x 13cm, then score and fold in half, creating a square blank. Attach blue patterned paper to cover the entire front, folding over the top crease. Secure in place with double-sided tape. Trim around the sides to neaten the edges.

2 Snip white card, 8cm x 10.5cm. Cut scrap card, 6cm square, to use as a template and stencil emboss this square in the top section of the white card.

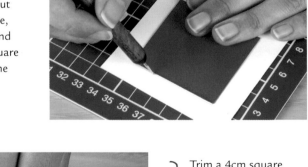

3 Trim a 4cm square from the middle of the embossed area. To find the centre point, draw faint pencil lines diagonally on the back of the card between the corners of the embossed shape. Stamp baby feet onto the reverse of blue patterned paper using a watermark ink pad.

Top Tip

Keep the gun moving with circular motions as you heat up the powder, so you don't overheat one spot – it should take 30 seconds.

4 Sprinkle the baby feet design with silver embossing powder, then activate it with the heat gun. Before setting the image, check that there are no stray specks of embossing powder as these will leave tiny silver dots. Trim, leaving a generous border.

7 On the front of the white card, stick a sliver of double-sided tape to hold the blue ric-rac in position and secure on the back, again using tape. This will stop the ribbon drooping when the button is attached. Attach this front panel centrally to the covered blue patterned card blank.

5 Mount the white embossed frame over the stamped image using double-sided tape. Ensure that the image is central in the window. Mount this panel to denim blue card, securing only at the top with a single strip of double-sided tape, leaving the bottom section free.

6 Thread narrow white ribbon through a polka dot button. Cut the ends at a sharp angle so that they can be easily passed through the button holes. Tie the ribbon in a double knot and put to one side.

8 To complete the card, add the polka dot button to the left of the blue ric-rac using diamond glaze glue. Hold in position for a minute so that the adhesive sets and holds the button firmly.

Enter the Dragon

Create a dramatic Oriental card that's perfect for every occasion. The central dragon image is repeated embossed using ultra-thick embossing powder, and mounted on red and gold card.

1 Stamp a Chinese lettering stamp onto black card and emboss in gold. Trim to 15cm x 4.5cm, then mount onto red, then gold card. Glue this panel to the left side of a 15cm square black blank. Wipe a clear embossing pad over a 10cm black card circle. Cover with ultra-thick gold embossing powder and heat.

2 Wipe ink over the embossed area, cover with powder and heat again. Repeat. While still hot, press a dragon stamp into it, removing it when cool. Tear around the embossed area.

3 Mount onto an 11cm red card circle, and edge with gold pen. Stick to the blank with sticky foam pads. Stamp and emboss three seals onto red card and cut out. Mount with foam pads over a length of wire.

Top Tip
Don't worry if the edges of the embossing are irregular – it adds to the oriental feel of the card.

TIME: 30 minutes
DESIGNER: Kay Webb

Frame Work

Use a brass stencil to emboss an elegant frame for this delicate floral design, made using easy stamping and embossing techniques and layering with contrasting coloured card.

TIME: 20 minutes
DESIGNER: Kay Webb

Top Tip

Mix textured and plain cards when layering to add even more interest to your card designs.

1 Cut olive green card, 21cm square, crease and fold in half. Ink a tall flower stamp using green, lilac and dark mauve brush markers and print onto white card. Trim to 6.5cm x 11cm and edge with a gold pen. Using a brass stencil, emboss a frame onto the white card.

2 Mount the stamped flower onto first blue then lilac card. Ink a greeting stamp with lilac brush marker and print in the bottom right corner of the white panel. Fix a swirl paper clip to the top right corner of the lilac card, then attach the flower panel to the olive green blank with double-sided tape.

3 Pierce a small hole in the spine near the base of the card. Twist together green, lilac and blue embroidery silks and thread through, wrap them around the blank and tie in a knot at the front. Stick a line of pale green crystals down the right side of the blank.

Touch of Frost

Use easy embossing techniques to make a fantastic layered snowflake medallion greeting, set against a pretty embossed border and snowflake vellum background.

Top Tip

For an ice-white card without the sparkles, use white embossing powder instead of clear, and leave out the glitter.

TIME: 55 minutes
DESIGNER: Jo Gratwick

1 Stamp a snowflake medallion five times in pearlescent ice-blue ink, then emboss with clear powder. Apply glue to small sections of the design at a time, and add icicle fairy dust fine glitter to the parts that will be seen when layered. When dry, cut out each outline slightly smaller than the last one, and layer with sticky foam pads, largest first.

2 Fold an A4 white hammered card blank in half and trim 6cm from the bottom. Emboss a snowflake design freehand or with a template along the fold. Accent with glitter glue. Leave to dry. Mark 9cm from the fold, along the top and bottom of the blank.

3 Measure the central point between them and trim a semi-circle to the right of this line, with a 5.5cm radius. Trim and stick white snowflake vellum behind the semi-circle and edge with glitter glue. Mount the layered snowflake centrally.

Diamonds Forever

Gold, black and lilac papers add a refined touch to this elegant design. Use an embossing tool and a floral stencil to create a pretty raised effect on this sparkling card.

Top Tip

Adding a second mount at a different angle using decorative toning paper adds extra interest and enhances the embossed image.

TIME: 40 minutes
DESIGNER: Dorothy Walsh

1 Emboss a floral design using a stencil or by hand, onto pale lilac card. To do this, place the stencil wrong-side down onto the wrong-side of the pale lilac. This will ensure the image will appear correctly on the right side. Press onto the edges of the stencil with an embossing tool in order to outline the image, then use the same technique to emboss the inner areas. Trim to 8.5cm square.

2 Layer onto textured gold, then black card. Cut floral decorative paper, 10cm square, and layer onto gold textured, then black card as before.

3 Fix the decorative paper square onto a textured white card blank, 14cm square. Stick the embossed image diagonally across the patterned square to finish.

All Aflutter

Show you care with this pretty card, embossed with a contemporary butterfly design. Repeat the same butterfly stencil to create a stylish patterned panel.

1 Fold an A5 white card in half and cut down the fold. Emboss two lines of squares on one piece of card with a stencil. Turn over and emboss on the other side of the card (in between the lines of squares) using a butterflies stencil. To emboss the designs, place the stencil the wrong side down, on the wrong side of the paper. Use an embossing tool to press into the edges of the stencil, creating a raised effect.

2 Trim the front of the card close to the line of squares and edge with gold pen. Stick the embossed panel onto textured white A5 folded card, creating a border on one side.

3 Add a silver metal butterfly over the embossed butterflies with strong glue to finish.

Top Tip
This card incorporates embossing on both sides of the plain white card to produce embossed and debossed (impressed) images.

TIME: 50 minutes

DESIGNER: Dorothy Walsh

Blue Rhapsody

Give a beloved female relative this charming greeting that she's sure to treasure. This pretty embossed flower basket will delight the recipient.

Top Tip
Embossing on vellum produces a different effect than on ordinary card, creating a white image on the coloured background.

TIME: 30 minutes
DESIGNER: Dorothy Walsh

1 Emboss a flower basket onto blue vellum, 12cm x 14.5cm, by hand or using a stencil. If you are using a stencil, place the stencil the wrong side up on the wrong side of the card. Use a small embossing tool to press down into the edges of the stencil and cover the whole of the stencil, creating a raised pattern on the right side of the card.

2 Tear a 1cm strip from the bottom edge and add a line with gold pen. Fold a 1.5cm strip of vellum over the folded edge of a pale grey A5 folded card and fix at the back.

3 Tie a bow in gold embroidery thread and stick onto the top left corner. Fix a crystal bead on top with PVA glue.

Golden Greeting

Brighten up somebody's day with a pretty card decorated with gorgeous sunflowers. The sunflower charm looks striking against the raised sunflower design.

1 Emboss a flower, by hand or using a stencil, onto cream card following the technique described in Step One on page 153. Trim to 5.5cm x 8cm. Round the corners, and edge with gold pen.

2 Layer onto mustard card edged with gold pen. Fix to the right side of folded cream card, 14.5cm square, and round the corners on the right side.

3 Stencil the flower design twice onto cream card, 5.5cm x 14.5cm, using butterscotch and green ink-pads.

4 Stick the stencilled design to the left side of the greeting, then add a silver sunflower charm and gold thread to decorate the embossed image.

Top Tip
Embossing and stencilling the same design onto separate pieces of toning card that have had their corners rounded, adds extra interest.

TIME: One hour
DESIGNER: Dorothy Walsh

Objet D'art

Inspired by Charles Rennie Mackintosh, this graceful floral card is a true masterpiece. The raised design adds an elegant feel to this stylish card.

Top Tip

Layering the embossed image on to black glossy card makes it stand out, while the gold hanging rod and ribbon creates the effect of a picture.

TIME: 40 minutes
DESIGNER: Dorothy Walsh

1 Emboss an Art Nouveau design by hand or using a stencil, onto pink card. Place the stencil the wrong side up on the wrong side of the card. Use an embossing tool to press down into the edges of the stencil.

2 Turn over, and stipple colours from raisin, aubergine and llight green ink-pads onto the central flower image.

3 Trim the image and layer onto black glossy card, then onto hammered gold card. Fix towards the bottom of an A5 folded white textured card blank.

4 Add a gold metal hanging rod with a tied gold organza ribbon above the embossed image to complete the card.

Stick 'em Up!

Create fabulous designs quickly and easily,
with the application of attractive
peel-offs

Stickers aren't just for kids any more, in fact there
is a wide range of peel-offs available that allow you
to add images, text or borders to your greetings.
They are so simple to apply, yet the end result
looks highly professional. Once you have removed
them all, the backing sheets can be used as reverse
designs or stencils – true value for money!

Charm School

This card is both funky and retro and
will appeal to all tastes and ages. It also
demonstrates the versatility of peel-offs; they
can be used to create backgrounds, motifs
and even 3D charms.

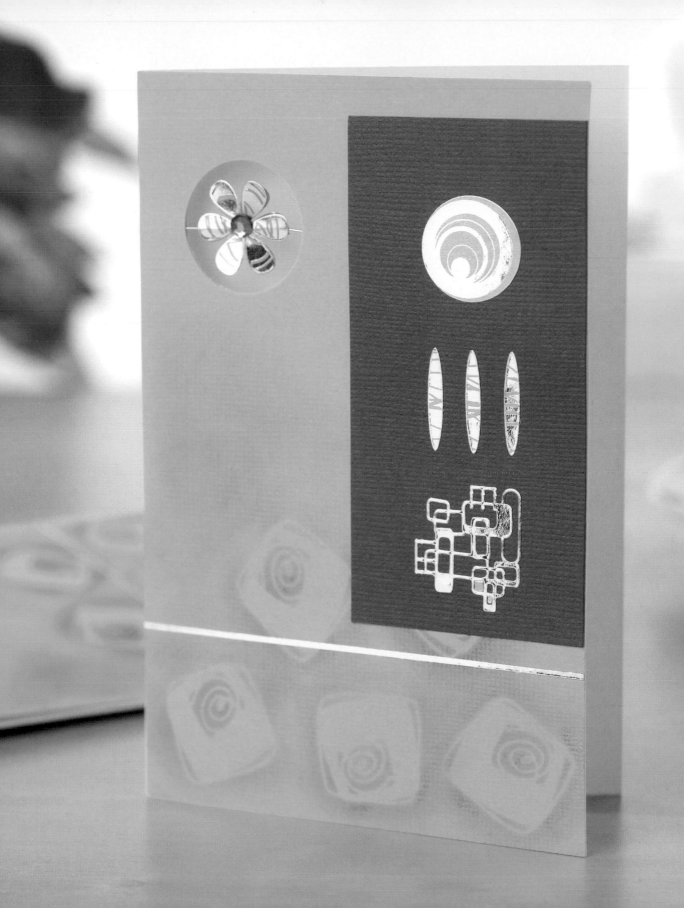

1 Select a peel-off to use for the backing pattern. Stick it to the back of your hand a few times to make it less tacky and easier to remove. Place in the desired position onto blue card, the same size as the blank, and press evenly and lightly.

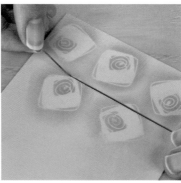

Top Tip
When applying peel-offs to card, place them lightly at first, so they can be lifted up and repositioned easily, if required. When you are happy with their placement, press them down firmly

You will need
White card blank

Mid-blue and mocha card

Retro peel-off stickers

Blue chalk

Medium circle punch

Flat-backed yellow gem

Silver craft wire

Cotton wool ball

TIME: 15 minutes

PROJECT DESIGNER: Karen Weiderhold

2 Rub a cotton wool ball over the blue chalk and then sweep the colour over the peel-off from the inside outwards. Don't rub too hard, it could lift the peel-off and smudge the design.

3 Lift the peel-off from the card and reapply to the next area for chalking. Repeat step 2 until you have added as many motifs as you need. Apply a silver line peel-off, 4.5cm from the base of the card.

4 Cut a length of wire measuring 7.5cm. Select two matching or reverse image peel-offs. Take one of these stickers and lie the wire across the centre of it, on the adhesive side. Stick the second peel-off over it, trapping the wire in between them.

6 Place the blue panel onto the blank, in line with the card face but do not adhere yet. Punch a circle on the top left-hand side through both layers. Set the blue piece aside.

7 Tape the wire of your 3D charm onto the white card front, so the charm appears in the circle. Glue the decorated blue card to the front of the greeting, hiding the charm wire and sandwiching it between the two layers.

5 When adhering the peel-offs together, align them carefully and press very lightly first. This way, if you make a mistake, the two can be taken apart easily, without damaging them. Once they are lined up properly, press firmly together.

8 Glue a yellow, flat-backed gem to the centre of the charm. Select more peel-offs and apply to brown card, 6.2cm x 11.2cm. Stick the rectangle onto the front of the card, 0.5cm above the silver line, against the right-hand edge.

Gift Token

Use peel-off stickers to create a fun greeting that's really easy-to-make and can be adapted to suit any theme or occasion. All you need are the right peel-offs!

1 Cut 21cm x 15cm of light orange card, and fold in half. Cut dark orange card, 15cm x 10.5cm, and carefully stick to the inside back of the blank, making sure all the edges are aligned.

2 Using a sharp craft knife over a cutting mat, draw and trim an aperture, 4cm x 11.5cm, from the front of the card blank. Open the card and lay out flat while cutting, to avoid marking the inside back of the greeting, and check the aperture is centred before you start cutting.

3 Cut acetate the same size as the aperture panel on the card. Use glue dots to attach it behind the aperture, then carefully peel off a series of gift stickers and position them on the acetate within the aperture.

Top Tip
After cutting your aperture with a craft knife, smooth the cut edges with a bone folder for a fine finish.

TIME: 20 minutes
DESIGNER: Jane Kharade

Layer Cake

Create an eye-catching display on a greeting using gold peel-off medallion stickers and brightly coloured card in several contrasting shades.

Top Tip

Lift peel-off stickers carefully from their backing paper using the tip of a craft knife.

TIME: 50 minutes

DESIGNER: Ann McColgan

1 Fix a peel-off border around the edges of a square pearlescent purple card blank. Create an insert from pale pink paper and attach to the blank.

2 Take a sheet of medallion peel-off stickers, and card in several contrasting colours, such as purple, pink and lilac. Peel off each medallion from the sheet and stick onto card. These will be layered on top of each other in size order, so vary the colours in the sequence you would like them to appear on the finished card.

3 Cut around each shape with a craft knife and assemble them together onto the blank, starting with the largest medallion. Use sticky foam pads to space the layers out from each other.

1 Trim thin paper, 8cm square, and fix to your card, slightly above the centre. Glue an image from festive wrapping in the centre. Cut four strips of doily, either straight or curved, to go along the edges of the inner square. Fix in place with a thin layer of glue.

2 Choose a large motif from the doily to go in the corners. Cut out four of these, and stick onto thin coloured paper. Leave to dry, then trim carefully around the edge. Fix one to each corner of the coloured paper.

3 Add a few gold flower motifs as highlights or to conceal the joins in the pieces of doily. You can also make a matching gift tag in the same way, then punch a hole at one end and thread through a ribbon.

Dainty Doily

Here's a fabulous idea for a festive card make. Transform a traditional tea time favourite into a delicate card decoration with a nostalgic twist.

Top Tip
Use tweezers when handling delicate material such as doily. This will prevent tearing and fingerprint marks.

TIME: 40 minutes

DESIGNER: Lucinda Ganderton

Check It Out!

Create your own Christmas greetings with a difference, using retro peel-off ribbon borders and plaid patterned paper in subtle shades of blue and green.

Top Tip
Create a matching gift tag by using a label punch and covering with the plaid paper. Finish with a matching ribbon peel-off sticker.

TIME: 30 minutes
DESIGNER: Françoise Read

1 Trim plaid patterned paper to 5cm x 15cm, and mount onto a white card blank, 8cm x 17.5cm. Stick two ribbon peel-offs across the card vertically and horizontally, positioning the bow as shown.

2 Add a tall tree peel-off to some green striped paper and carefully cut out with scissors. Decorate with peel-off lines, or mark with blue felt tip. Trim blue paper, 2.5cm x 7cm, add two peel-off lines and mount onto the card, just below the mid-point.

3 Use sticky foam pads to add the tree to the blue panel, and place a star above the tip of the tree. Fix the peel-off greeting below the bow on the ribbon line. Finish off by adding two brads on the right side of the blue panel.

1 Use a gold gel pen to outline some daisy and heart stickers on the backing sheet. Allow to dry. Lift and place the shapes onto pale orange card. Use coloured pencils to shade over some mesh wire to achieve the netted effect shown here.

2 Highlight the centres with a gel pen. Trim, rounding the corners, then mount onto pale green, slightly larger card. Cover part of a white card, 7cm x 16.5cm, with paper, adding a pale green strip.

3 Mount the daisy panel using 3D sticky foam. Die-cut the spade and trowel, or draw a freehand version. Shade using coloured pencils. Tie handles together with ribbon and fix onto the blank. With a gel pen, colour two holographic dots and use as brads.

Amber Nectar

You can combine peel-off stickers with clever shading techniques to make stunning greetings like this daisy card that's sure to appeal to a gardener.

Top Tip

Getting a symmetrical look when rounding card edges by hand is tricky. Invest in a paper punch to eliminate trial and error.

TIME: 30 minutes

DESIGNER: Françoise Read

Pretty in Pink

Create a simple yet attractive flower design embellished with patterned papers. The flower is made from circles of card with a drawn on stitching line.

Top Tip
Fix a treasured photo inside to make a permanent display card.

TIME: 30 minutes
DESIGNER: Karen Wiederhold

1 Cut some soft green card, 32cm x 18cm. Score down it 7.5cm from the left edge, 10cm from the right edge, then fold into three sections. Shape five circles from pink card, 6cm in diameter, and one circle in yellow card, 3.5cm in diameter. Dust with pink and white chalks.

2 Trim striped patterned paper, 10cm x 7cm, glue to the right front flap, and add a strip of ric-rac down the centre. Stick lime dotted paper to the left front flap.

3 Arrange and fix the pink circles into a flower shape. Add a button sticker to the yellow circle and finish with pink thread. Draw in stitch marks with a zig writer pen on the petals. Attach the flower to the left front flap, with half of it over the edge.

1 Cut a rectangle of
50 x 33 squares in silver
from a mosaic sticker sheet.
Fix this onto the middle of
a slightly larger white card
blank. With a pricking tool,
place coloured inlays onto
the silver mosaic background.
Prick out a medium-sized
decorative frame as shown.

2 Pick a suitable sized
flower peel-off motif
and a frame to go in the
centre of your mosaic frame.
Arrange both onto white
card. Colour in the petals
and border with felt-tip pens
and trim the card into an
oval shape to fit inside the
mosaic frame.

3 Stick the oval card in
place on the card mount
using double-sided tape or
3D sticky foam pads for a
raised effect.

Mosaic Frame

Here's a fun cardmaking technique to try:
creating a mosaic border for your greeting
from a sticker sheet. The results are fabulous
and well worth the effort.

Top Tip

Use a flower stamp in the centre
of the design and ink it with water-
colour for a different but highly
effective look.

Time: One hour
Designer: Isle Scheffer

Let's Fly Away

White peel-off butterflies set against bright red card make a dramatic combination on this striking anniversary card – need we say more?

Top Tip
It works just as well to use 3D adhesive dots instead of 3D sticky foam pads for attaching a layer or motif. Both will raise it and make it stand out.

TIME: 45 minutes
DESIGNER: Wendy Horrod

1 Peel off three butterfly motifs from a peel-off sheet and fix to red card. Leave to stick for a few moments before trimming around the shapes, being careful when cutting around the antenna.

2 Cut a white background, 12cm x 4.7cm, and layer onto a gold rectangle, leaving a 1mm border. Mount onto a folded blank, 8cm x 17.5cm, using sticky foam pads. Punch out small red dots and attach to each corner with PVA glue.

3 Pick up each butterfly and bend the wings slightly before fixing them to the mounted panel with sticky foam pads. Finish with a white peel-off greeting, pressed down onto a red strip, and mount underneath the central image.

Artful Apertures

Create windows in your cardmaking
with some crafty cutting to show off
more of your handiwork

Aperture cards can literally add a whole new
dimension to your greetings. Simply by cutting a
'window' in the front face, or even just trimming
a portion of it away, you can reveal a design
on the inside that is just as gorgeous as what's
on top. Use photographs, printed papers or
embellishments to provide a wonderful surprise.

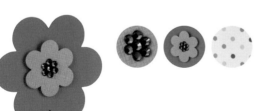

Heat Wave

This greeting uses a sizzling three-colour
block paper and matching card – perfect
for a summer celebration! Part of the card
front is trimmed away to reveal the inside
flap decorated with the three-colour paper.

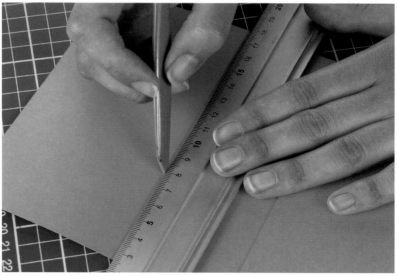

1 Cut and score a portrait A6 blank from tangerine cardstock. Trim off 2cm vertically down the right-hand side using a scalpel and metal ruler, revealing the inside flap of the card.

You will need

Raspberry red polka dot paper and three-colour block paper

Tangerine, orange and bubblegum colour card

Large and medium flower punches

Volcano crystals

Crystal applicator wand

Pink and orange narrow ribbon

Scalpel

Metal ruler

Double-sided tape

3D sticky foam pads

TIME: 15 minutes

PROJECT DESIGNER: Tracey Daykin-Jones

2 Trim a section of three squares from the colour-block paper and attach to the inside using double-sided tape. When sticking large sections of paper to card, peel off half the backing; when happy with the positioning, remove the remainder.

3 Trim a section of polka dot paper and attach to the front of the card so that it covers the entire card, fold around the crease and secure in place with double-sided tape. Trim the three sides of the card to neaten the edges.

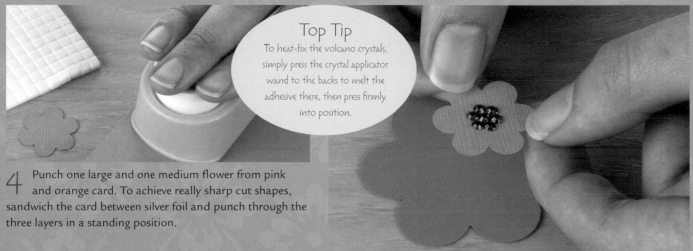

Top Tip
To heat-fix the volcano crystals, simply press the crystal applicator wand to the backs to melt the adhesive there, then press firmly into position.

4 Punch one large and one medium flower from pink and orange card. To achieve really sharp cut shapes, sandwich the card between silver foil and punch through the three layers in a standing position.

5 Fix a single volcano crystal to the centre of the small pink flower and add the remaining six gems around it in a flower shape. Attach the pink flower to the centre of the orange flower using several 3D sticky foam pads for extra security.

6 Cut a 1cm slit vertically midway down the centre of the card using a scalpel and metal ruler. Gently push through the two ends of a folded pink ribbon to form a leaf. Secure the ribbon in position on the inside of the blank with tape.

7 Stick a length of narrow orange ribbon vertically down the centre of the card, concealing the slit where the pink ribbon has been inserted. Secure with a piece of narrow double-sided tape and trim the end at an attractive angle.

8 To complete the card, add the layered flower section to the top of the orange ribbon, so that the ends are hidden. Use sticky pads to fix the bloom in place, giving the design a lovely three-dimensional effect.

True Blue

Conjure up the effect of pretty snowflakes floating silently against a dark blue sky on a gorgeous greeting made by transferring foil snowflakes on to acetate.

1 Fold a 21cm x 15cm turquoise card blank in half. Cut a strip of dark blue card, 15cm x 10.5cm and carefully stick down the centre of the inside back of the card blank.

2 Use a sharp craft knife over a cutting mat to cut an aperture, 5.5cm x 11cm in the front of the turquoise blank. Open the card and lay out flat while doing this to prevent marking the back, and check the aperture will be centred before you start cutting.

3 Cut some acetate, 21cm x 15cm, and transfer a series of silver snowflakes foil motifs onto it. Position them so they can be seen through the aperture. Fix the acetate to the inside front of the card with repositional glue dots.

Top Tip
You can create a more opaque effect by using a coloured acetate instead of a transparent one.

TIME: 25 minutes
DESIGNER: Jane Kharade

Party Time

Fresh lime and vibrant primary colours make a bold and original statement at Christmas. Make this card for a special friend – it's sure to stand out on the shelf.

TIME: 20 minutes

DESIGNER: Net Simpson

1 Fold a 21cm x 15cm lime green card blank in half. Draw a 12cm square on the front and mark out four small square apertures inside it, with a 1cm border between them and cut them out. Using hand-drawn templates, cut a bauble from blue card, a present from red card, a green tree and a yellow star.

2 Add a light blue stripe and silver detail to the bauble. Place a clear dome sticker over the top, and trim the edges. Using a dark green pencil, shade in the tree and cover the trunk in brown paper. Highlight the star edges with orange and add a ribbon to the present.

3 Hang the bauble with ribbon at the first window. Fix the tree and star over the second and third windows. Fix the present at an angle behind the last window.

Birdie Song

Our chirpy robin is sure to send plenty of festive cheer during the Christmas season. He looks gorgeous against a pyramid card decorated with gold glitter ivy motifs.

1 Using the template on page 254, make a pyramid-shaped greetings blank from cream card. Transfer an ivy motif around the top and the base, then sprinkle with micro glitter.

2 Cut a triangular panel from cream card smaller than the centre front panel on the blank. Stick onto gold mirrored card, trim to leave a narrow border and fix to the front of the pyramid blank with glue dots. Transfer a large robin motif onto cream card and sprinkle with red micro glitter. Cut out leaving a narrow white border and stick onto the cream panel with 3D sticky foam pads.

3 You can also make your design into a gift-tag by punching a hole in the corner of the folded card and tying gold and red tinsel to the top.

Top Tip

Holly alternative: stamp a holly or leaf image onto the card and then highlight using green glitter pens.

TIME: 40 minutes
DESIGNER: Anita Brooks

Strip Trees

Use abstract shapes to form a tree and colourful brads for the decorations on this fun, retro-style greeting. It's ideal for using up any leftover papers you may have.

TIME: 40 minutes
DESIGNER: Paula Pascual

1 Trim red card to A5 size. Crease to form a gate-fold blank, using a folding board. Cover the two front flaps with striped paper, cut slightly smaller all round.

2 Cut random strips of green card and decorate with brads in several shades. If you wish to cover the split ends of the brads on the back, attach another piece of green card over them on the back.

3 Fix the first green strip to the left front flap of the card with glue, so that half of it hangs over the right edge. Fix the second green strip to the right flap so that half of it hangs over the left edge. Fix the two other strips on alternate sides to form a funky, retro tree design. Add your message on a final green strip across the bottom.

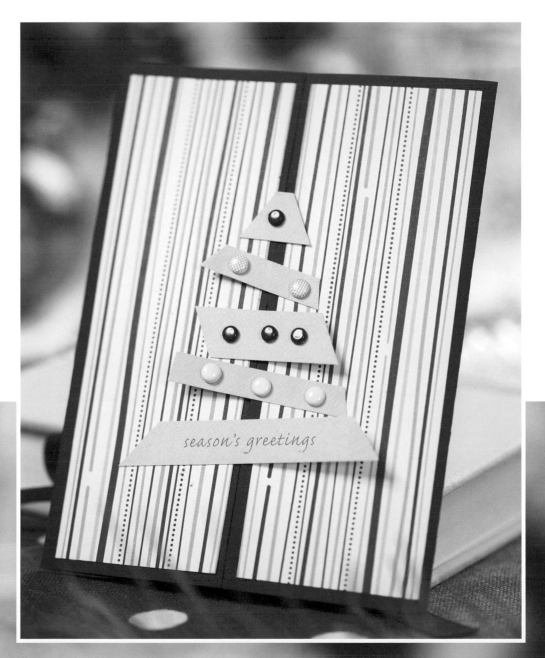

season's greetings

Scent With Love

Let the sweet aroma of dried lavender infuse your home this Christmas from this delightful card that has lavender concealed behind heart-shaped apertures.

Top Tip
Handmade paper is much easier to tear if you paint your tearing line first with a thin wet paintbrush.

TIME: 40 minutes

DESIGNER: Corinne Bradd

1 Fold a pre-cut heart aperture card and push the shapes out. Cut a strip of purple handmade paper large enough to cover the holes with 1cm extra all around. Lightly apply glue around each aperture on the inside of the card. Press the handmade paper onto this, pushing it through the apertures to a depth of 5mm.

2 Open out the card and fill the indents with dried lavender. Glue another piece of handmade paper over the top of the last piece to seal in the lavender.

3 Trim a 2cm strip of striped fabric and fray one long edge. Cut a strip of handmade paper, 1.5cm wide, dampen one long edge and tear carefully down it to give a frayed effect. Glue first the handmade paper then the fabric to the left hand side of the card, frayed edges facing out. Neaten both pieces top and bottom to finish.

Four Seasons

Use nature as your inspiration for a card celebrating the turn of the seasons. Each one is represented by pretty embellishments on a fluted card aperture.

TIME: One hour
DESIGNER: Glennis Gilruth

1 Cut turquoise folded card, 8cm x 18cm and trim the opening edge to give a wavy effect. Using a small plier punch, make holes along this edge and add white whipping stitches in ultra-fine paper yarn. Pierce a hole in the top left corner with a medium plier punch and thread with strands of paper yarn, with a greeting scrap attached.

2 Trim four 2.5cm squares of white fluted card and decorate with curls of craft wire and seed beads to represent the buds of spring. Use flower shapes and beads for summer and a glittered and trimmed skeleton leaf with sequins for autumn. Finally, use a punched snowflake with a gem in the centre for winter. Fix the squares to the card using 3D sticky foam pads for a lovely raised effect.

Pretty Posies

Make this charming greeting for someone special using a stamped motif. They'll love opening it up to discover you've made three bouquets for them instead of just one!

Cut 30cm x 15cm green card. Mark and fold at 7.5cm, 15cm and 20cm intervals, in a concertina blank. Trim striped paper to fit the front and inside back pages. Stick with double-sided tape leaving a narrow green border.

2 Print a flowers-in-a-vase stamp three times on white card using black ink, then shade with water-colour crayons. Cut out using a large circle template, or punch.

3 Stick the first circle to the inside back of the card, then fix the other two circles to the front and middle inside panel, making them lie over each other. Tie co-ordinating ribbon around the front in a bow and fix a small strip of green card decorated with pink crystal hearts to the front.

Top Tip
Instead of stamping the middle circle with a flower image, stamp a circular greeting and apply water-colour crayons.

TIME: 30 minutes
DESIGNER: Kay Webb

Window Dressing

Create a stylish multi-layered card using patterned papers and card in toning shades, and top it off with a pretty floral stamp image tied with a ribbon.

Top Tip
Remember that a card like this one will need a larger envelope to accommodate the raised design.

TIME: 30 minutes
DESIGNER: Kay Webb

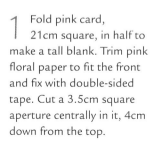

1 Fold pink card, 21cm square, in half to make a tall blank. Trim pink floral paper to fit the front and fix with double-sided tape. Cut a 3.5cm square aperture centrally in it, 4cm down from the top.

2 Snip pink striped paper, 18.5cm x 8cm, and make a 5cm square aperture centrally in it, 2.5cm down from the top. Mount onto slightly larger plain pink card and cut out round the window with a craft knife to leave a small border as shown.

3 Ink a hydrangea stamp using pink and green brush markers and print onto white card. Cut out leaving a fine border all round. Tie a small pink bow around the stalk and fix to the card with 3D sticky foam pads.

Stunning Stencils

Paint perfect images onto your cards every time, with the aid of stencils

Stencilling is a simple and effective method of decorating paper, card, fabrics and even walls. Paint is applied over the top of a template or stencil, leaving an image on the underlying surface when the stencil is lifted off. You can create intricate effects with stencils by building up layers of images and cutting a separate stencil for each layer.

Rain Dance

This stencil design has two layers; one for the outer shape and another for the central droplet. By using three shades of turquoise, you can achieve a subtle, shaded effect that tones with the white background.

You will need

Turquoise and white acrylic or stencil paint

Aqua and white card

Sponge, dauber or brush

Spray glue

Low tack tape

Scalpel or hot cutter

Cutting mat or board

Acetate or stencil film

3D sticky foam pads

Clear, flat-backed gems

TIME: 45 minutes

PROJECT DESIGNER: Sharon Bennett

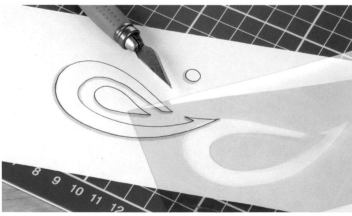

1 Cut a white card piece, 18.5cm x 22cm, score and fold in half. Draw a simple droplet shape on a piece of card, then draw the outer border using the main picture on page 180 as a guide. Lay the stencil film or acetate over the top.

Top Tip

When finished with the stencils, wash them clean while the paint is still fresh and wet. It will come off easily, without the risk of damaging them, and they will last longer.

2 Use a proper cutting mat with a scalpel, or board if you have a hot cutter. Cut out the stencil and coat the back lightly with spray glue – enough to make tacky, but not to fix permanently.

3 Position the stencil onto the right side of the blank. Use the photograph to help with positioning the droplet on the card. Pour turquoise paint into a palette or saucer, mix some with a little white and keep separate, then mix a third tone of turquoise that is even paler.

4 Never overload the brush or sponge, always dab onto spare paper first to get rid of any excess paint. This way you will achieve delicate prints. Shading looks good if the paint is applied lighter to one side. Adding a colour over another makes a great effect.

6 Move the stencil around until you have filled the whole blank with droplets. Add the outer border first before stencilling the droplet centres, using the dark turquoise paint. Allow each of your images to dry thoroughly before applying the next one.

7 Stencil three droplet centres in a horizontal line onto white card, one in each of the three tones of turquoise. Mount onto aqua card. Trim to leave an aqua border at the top and bottom, but not on the sides.

5 Apply the two lighter tones of paint to the outer area of the droplet with the dauber. Use the medium shade on the rounded end, and the palest colour at the tip. Let them fuse over each other when they join. Use a separate dauber for each shade.

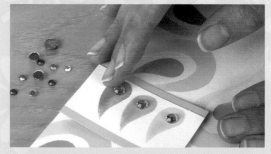

8 Mount the decorated panel on the front of the blank, using sticky foam pads so that it is slightly raised from the surface. Add a clear gem to each droplet to finish.

Fairy Cake

This scrumptious-looking greeting made using two pretty shades of acrylic paint and the template on page 254, is sure to make you feel peckish!

Top Tip
Tape paper over the top part of the stencil when sponging the bottom half. This will prevent any gold paint accidentally marking the top.

TIME: 30 minutes
DESIGNER: Jill Alblas

1 Print out your chosen message or greeting on a computer and trim to size. Use double-sided tape to stick the greeting 1.5cm from the base of a tall red card blank. Cut a 5cm square of red gingham fabric, fray all round the edges and tape it centrally 1.5cm away from the top of the blank.

2 Trace the fairy cake template from page 254 onto card and cut out using a sharp craft knife. Tape the stencil onto white card and sponge the bottom half with gold acrylic paint and the top half with pink paint (see page 183). Carefully remove the stencil and if necessary touch up any untidy edges with a fine paintbrush.

3 Cut out the stencilled fairy cake design, leaving a border of white card showing all round. Fix it in the centre of the gingham fabric square using 3D sticky foam pads, then attach a red pom pom cherry above it with a glue dot.

National Grid

Stencil hearts and stars onto squares cut from contrasting shades of card to make an attractive simple greeting that will suit many different occasions.

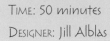

Top Tip

Wipe each stencil with a damp sponge after each application of silver paint. Dry it before beginning the next square.

TIME: 50 minutes
DESIGNER: Jill Alblas

1 Choose three shades of card that contrast well together, for example lilac, yellow and magenta. Trim three, 3cm squares from each colour card to make a total of nine squares.

2 Draw a simple heart and star on card. Check they are the right size to fit inside your squares then cut out using a sharp craft knife over a cutting mat. Use the card heart and star as templates to cut two stencils into acetate or stencil film.

3 Use your heart stencil to sponge a heart in the centre of five of the coloured squares, and your star stencil to sponge a heart on four squares with silver acrylic paint. Fix the stencilled shapes in a block, on the front of a square blank with glue dots or craft glue.

Lazy Daisy

Brighten someone's day with this charming and cheerful flower card stencilled in orange and pink paint. Add your own special greeting along the stem.

Top Tip
If you don't have any acetate, sponge directly onto the card blank for a flatter but equally colourful finish.

TIME: 50 minutes
DESIGNER: Jill Alblas

1 Trace the daisy stencil template from page 254 onto acetate or stencil film and use a sharp craft knife to cut it out. Cut two squares, 6.5cm from thick acetate with a craft knife. Tape the stencil centrally over one of the acetate pieces and sponge in orange acrylic paint. Remove the stencil and if necessary, touch up the edges with a fine brush.

2 Repeat using bright pink acrylic paint on the second acetate square. Tape the stem and leaf stencil onto the centre of a tall card blank and sponge in green. Leave to dry, then hand write or use rub-down lettering to add a greeting running parallel with the stencilled stem.

3 Place a small double-sided tab in the centre, on the back of the orange daisy and stick it at the top of the blank. Attach the pink flower on top, but a different way up. Glue a crystal cabouchon in the centre of the pink daisy.

Picture Perfect

Use simple silk painting resist techniques to create a stunning abstract card your friends will love. They'll probably want to frame it afterwards!

TIME: One hour
DESIGNER: Sally Southern

Top Tip
Don't buy special silk stretching frames – a simple wooden picture frame with the glass removed will do just as well.

1 Cut silk to the size of a small frame and attach using silk pins, stretching it as tight as possible. Trace the template on page 254 onto the reverse of the silk in vanishing pen. Turn the frame right side up and go over the design carefully with gutta outline. Try to keep the lines even and not too thick.

2 Leave to dry before you begin painting. Pick up only a tiny amount of paint on the brush as it will spread very quickly over the surface. The colours can be mixed and blended on the silk as the gutta will prevent the dyes running into each other. Leave for 30 minutes to dry, then embellish with further small dots of gutta.

3 When this has set, remove the silk from the frame and trim the edges. Mount the fabric onto an aperture card blank, using double-sided tape to hold it in place. Draw a border on the front in gutta and glue on iridescent sequins.

Retro Revival

Paint bright swirling shapes onto white card to create fabulous looking motifs. This would make a funky looking Valentines card.

1 Transfer the design from the template on page 253, using tracing paper and a soft pencil. Colour with acrylic paint in fuchsia, apricot and yellow shades. Leave to dry.

2 Trim pink card and fold to make a tall thin blank. Cut or punch a patterned heart, pierce a hole at the top and thread through magenta ribbon. Fix to the centre of the blank, allowing the heart to hang free. Embellish the ribbon with dots of pink outliner.

3 For an alternative look, cut and fold a tall white card blank. Cut a patterned rectangle and divide into three sections. Glue each piece onto the greeting, one above the other in order, with equal spacing between the three parts.

TIME: 30 minutes
DESIGNER: Sharon Bennett

Bunnies at Play

Create an irresistible greeting by stencilling the springtime bunny from page 254 onto card and colouring him in soft shades of acrylic paint. What a cutie he is!

TIME: 40 minutes
DESIGNER: Sharon Bennett

Top Tip
You can make a shaped card, by copying the bunny onto a square blank towards the open edge, then trimming around the outline near the edge.

1 Trace the bunny pattern from page 254 onto white card. With a small brush, start to apply the acrylic colours, beginning with the rabbit's fur. This is a mixture of burnt amber with a dab of yellow and white. Test on scrap paper first to ensure a good match. Add a little water in order to soften the lines and create a gradual shaded effect.

2 Paint the middle of the ears and the jacket in pale pink. The flowers are pink, yellow and blue, with magenta centres, and leaves in dark green. Outline the bunny shape in dark brown, using a thin brush.

3 Make a wash of pastel pink and sweep onto a side-folded white blank, using a wide brush. Do not cover the whole card, but leave a slightly ragged edge. Fix the rabbit motif halfway down, using 3D sticky foam pads. Add two individual flowers in the same way.

1 Fold a purple card blank, 30cm x 20.5cm. Use a sharp craft knife over a cutting mat to trim a rectangular aperture, 7cm x 11.5cm. Draw a template onto white card using the photo as a guide. Trim acetate, 9cm x 13.5cm, lay centrally over your template and tape in place.

2 Carefully follow the lines with outliner paste and leave to dry overnight. Fill in the middle section with violet and turquoise glass paints. Stipple the excess with a brush. Cover the background with a heavier coating of ultramarine.

3 Run a continuous glue line along the unpainted edges. Fix to the inside of the aperture. Add an insert of white paper to the centre of the card to finish.

Under Glass

For a gorgeous stained glass effect, use glass paints on acetate following a simple line template and place your design behind a card aperture when dry.

Top Tip
When drawing straight lines with outliner paste, touch the nozzle to the acetate. Squeeze and lift the tube, pulling the line along until you reach the end.

TIME: 40 minutes
DESIGNER: Jane Kharade

Magic Numbers

It's easy to create a designer look using three stylish images cut from different shades of vellum arranged against a plain white card background.

Top Tip
You can buy both plain and patterned vellum in an exciting range of colours, which are perfect for a simple design like this one.

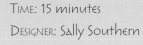

TIME: 15 minutes
DESIGNER: Sally Southern

congratulations

1 Trace around the three templates from page 254, and use them to cut out two flowers from translucent paper, one in lime green and one in turquoise. Trace the leaf shape from page 254 and cut out from brown paper.

2 Arrange the flowers onto a white card blank, 9cm x 11.5cm, so that they overlap each other and jut out beyond the edge of the card. Stick them in place with vellum glue and trim excess.

3 Fix the leaf shape on top of the blooms, near to the spine of the greeting. Add a metal charmed greeting to finish off your card.

Quick Quilling

Curl and coil narrow paper strips into pretty motifs ready to add dimensional detail to your cards

Quilling is a historic art that involves rolling, shaping and pinching narrow strips of paper into delicate coils to form a variety of three-dimensional designs. The craft has been refined by today's paper crafters to create striking effects. The basic coils themselves can be manipulated into a variety of shapes, from squares and rectangles to tear-drops and stars.

Gardener's World

This greeting celebrates the cycle of gardening, from the seed to the seedling and then to the flower. The frilly blooms are deceptively easy to make and the seedlings will appeal to all types of gardeners.

You will need

3mm wide quilling paper: bright green, light green, yellow and brown

10mm wide quilling paper: light orange, medium orange and dark orange

2mm wide quilling paper: black

Brown, silver, green and blue card

Orange patterned paper

Quilling tool

Fringing tool

Green card blank, 14.5cm square

3D sticky foam pads

PVA glue

TIME: 40 minutes

PROJECT DESIGNER: Elizabeth Moad

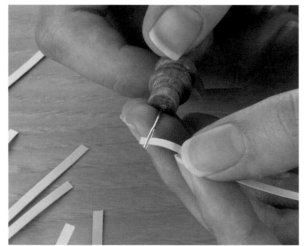

1 Take a 10cm length of 3mm wide bright green paper and insert 3mm between the prongs of a quilling tool. Holding this in one hand and the strip in the other, turn the tool round and round, coiling the paper as you go.

2 Once the end of the strip has been reached, remove the quilling tool and add a dot of white PVA to the end of the paper. Release the coil very slightly and glue the end in place. With your fingertips, pinch the coil into a teardrop shape.

3 Make eight more coils. Take one tear-drop, place a dot of PVA onto the rounded end, and attach to a 3cm length of 3mm wide bright green paper. Glue another coil on the other side of the strip. Hold each in place for five seconds while the glue dries.

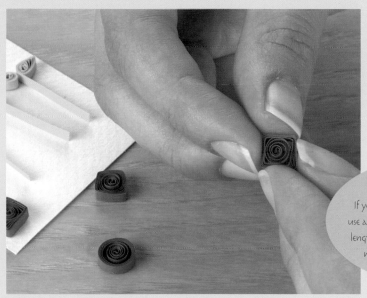

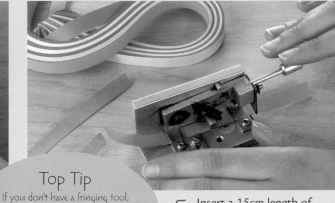

Top Tip
If you don't have a fringing tool, use a small pair of scissors to fringe a length of paper, holding the uncut margin with a bull dog clip.

4 Take a 20cm length of 3mm wide brown paper and coil as before. Glue the end in place and with your fingers, pinch into a square shape. Make three more of these and glue a seedling to each one. Attach to green card, 5.5cm square.

5 Insert a 15cm length of 10mm wide orange paper into a fringing tool. Move the handle up and down continuously so that the tool cuts the strip, making a fringe. The movement draws the paper through the tool as it goes.

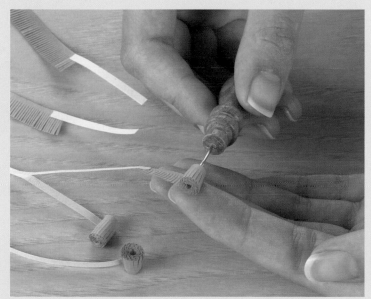

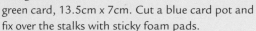

7 Once you reach the green paper, stop coiling and fix in place. Fan the petals out to reveal the yellow. Make four more flowers in various shades of orange, and fix to green card, 13.5cm x 7cm. Cut a blue card pot and fix over the stalks with sticky foam pads.

6 Take the fringed section out and stick a 4cm yellow length, 3mm wide, to one end and a 3mm wide light green strip, 10cm long to the other. These are glued to the non-fringed margin of the orange. Insert the yellow paper into the quilling tool and start making a tight coil.

8 Make a tight coil, using brown paper 2cm x 5cm, and glue to a 4cm strip of brown card. Cut a spade shape from silver card. With 2mm wide black, 2cm lengths, form 12 tight coils and stick to green card, 3.5cm x 5.5cm. Fold orange paper for the seed packet. Fix everything to the green card blank.

Let's Twist Again

Quilling is an ideal technique for Christmas cards – especially if you use paper edged with silver or gold. Here's a fun idea, for quick festive makes.

TIME: 25 minutes

DESIGNER: Elizabeth Moad

1 Create three circles in mauve, green and blue card. Add two strips of 2mm wide purple paper to the mauve bauble. Make 20 tight coils using 5cm lengths of 2mm wide blue quilling paper edged with silver, and glue between the lines in a zigzag.

2 For the green bauble, make 13 tight coils using 10cm lengths of red 2mm paper. Attach to the card in two curved lines. Spread glitter glue between and leave to dry overnight.

3 Fix two strips of purple paper to the blue bauble. Make three loose coils using 2mm wide dark purple paper and stick between the lines. Cut three, 2cm squares of silver card and fold in half. Round off the top corners on each and make a hole in the middle of the fold with a needle, and thread with looped silver wire. Stick over the bauble with double-sided tape. Fix the baubles to a cream card blank with sticky foam pads.

Oriental Charm

Curling two different shades of paper up together gives a lovely two-tone effect. This is used to create the petals on this elegant Japanese-inspired floral design.

Top Tip
Quilling papers are available in many different colours, but if you can find the colour you want – cut your own!

TIME: 15 minutes
DESIGNER: Elizabeth Moad

1 Tear a strip of Japanese handmade paper, 20cm x 3.5cm. Attach to a pale blue card blank, 18.5cm x 7cm. Punch out a circle from cream card.

2 Put a 20cm length of pale blue 3mm wide quilling paper with one of darker blue. Place both ends into a quilling tool and make a coil with the pale blue outside. Glue the end in position and pinch into a tear-drop shape.

3 Make four more tear-drops in this way, with the pale blue outside. Take a 10cm length of both papers and adhere end to end. Make a tight coil with the darker blue on the outside. Attach these to the circle and mount onto the patterned panel on the blank.

Wings of Love

Celebrate the beauty of nature with a pretty quilled greeting. You can create many different effects by allowing the paper coils to unravel a little before you stick them.

Top Tip

Dab a spot of glue to the outside of the quilling paper after slotting on the quilling tool (not the side that will rest next to the tool). This will stop the coil unravelling when easing the tool off.

TIME: 35 minutes

DESIGNER: Elizabeth Moad

1 Cut strips of 3mm wide mauve quilling paper of varying lengths. Use a quilling tool to make loose coils. Glue these onto light purple card, 11cm square. Cut five leaves from grey paper, score the centres and attach.

2 For the butterfly, cut strips of 3mm wide cream paper, two 25cm and two 35cm long. Make closed coils, allow the outer layers to uncoil a little and pinch into tear-drop shapes as shown. Cut a 4cm piece of 3mm wide black paper for the body, coil and pinch flat.

3 Take 3cm of black and cut down the middle for 2cm. Curl each tiny strand, then glue to the pinched coil. Stick the body to the card first, then the wings.

4 Make a smaller butterfly with two 25cm lengths of 3mm wide paper and two 15cm pieces, for the wings. Keep the body measurements the same. Fix to the card and mount onto a purple blank.

Winged Wonders

Pretty as a picture, this candy coloured greeting featuring dainty quilled butterflies and flowers on a mauve background card is perfect for a special celebration.

TIME: 35 minutes
DESIGNER: Elizabeth Moad

Top Tip
Use a needle quilling tool to create a tight coil with a very fine hole at the centre.

1 Fringe three 15cm lengths of 10mm wide paper, in three purple shades. Take one strip and attach 4cm of 3mm wide yellow paper to one end, and 10cm of light green to the other. Coil the arrangement tightly, starting with the yellow. Glue in place when the green is reached. Repeat for the others and fix to a lilac gate-fold blank. Add green stems and leaves from 12cm and 6cm strips, cut to a point.

2 Form two closed loose coils from 30cm lengths of 3mm wide pink metallic edged paper. Pinch one end. Repeat with two 20cm strips of the same paper. Make a closed loose coil from 10cm of brown 2mm wide paper. Pinch both ends. Snip the centre of a 2cm brown strip, down the length for 1.5cm. Curl the antennae and fix.

3 Glue body onto blank and attach wings. Make more butterflies, varying the lengths of paper used.

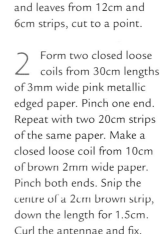

1 Using a quilling tool and a strip of 3mm yellow paper, form a tight coil and glue the end. To make a daisy, snip 12mm wide purple paper at regular intervals, leaving 3mm uncut. Coil around the yellow centre.

2 Ease from the quilling tool, and open gently. Make two more flowers this way. Cut three, 3mm green strips in half, make six loose coils, and glue the ends. Pinch into leaves.

3 Layer a rectangle of yellow paper over lilac checked paper and stick onto the centre of a deckle-edged card blank. Attach three 3mm green paper stalks and fix the daisies and leaves with double-sided tape.

4 Punch a butterfly from lilac glitter paper and glue in the top left corner. Make a tag from purple card and write a message on it. Pierce a hole and thread with wire coil. Fix with a green brad and a sticky foam pad.

Top Tip
Tear the end of the quilling paper instead of cutting it. This produces a more subtle join as the paper will taper off more.

Daisy Days
These purple and yellow quilled daisies make a wonderful greeting to send to someone special. Add greeting to a tag punched from matching card.

TIME: 30 minutes
DESIGNER: Lesley Price

Shrinking Violet

Fashion gorgeous purple flowers from fringed quilling paper and mount on matching card decorated with patterned vellum to make this lovely greeting.

TIME: 15 minutes
DESIGNER: Elizabeth Moad

Top Tip
Place bubble wrap inside the envelope when posting cards with fringed flowers.

1 Fringe a 10mm wide purple paper strip using a fringing tool or scissors, then cut a piece 15cm long. Glue a 10cm length of green 3mm wide paper to one end, and a 4cm section of 3mm wide yellow paper to the other.

2 Coil the length tightly, starting with the yellow, and stopping when the green is reached. Dab glue with a cocktail stick where the coil meets the stem and hold until dry. Use your fingers to spread the fringe into a flower shape. Make three purple flowers in this way.

3 Cut a circle 7.5cm in diameter from purple card. Attach the three flowers and trim the stems so they fit inside. Cut printed vellum, 12cm square, and fold in half. Affix to a purple card blank, 12cm square, matching the fold on both and adding glue to the back only. Mount the circle centrally over the vellum and card using sticky foam pads.

Sunny Side Up

Make a bright summery quilled card featuring a beautiful yellow sunflower made from yellow tear-drop shapes and a stunning fringed brown paper centre.

1 Take a 40cm length of dark brown quilling paper and insert into a fringing tool. Take a 20cm length of lighter brown quilling paper and fringe it as well. Join the pieces end to end, and insert them into a quilling tool. Coil them up tightly together so that the lighter brown paper is on the inside, then secure in place with a dot of PVA glue.

2 Attach the quilled circle to cream card, 7cm square. Make 24, tear-drop shaped petals from 20cm lengths of 3mm wide yellow quilling paper and glue in two layers around the flower centre as shown.

3 Mount centrally onto an orange card blank. Cut a small slit in the fold, thread yellow ribbon through, tie in a knot and trim the ends.

Top Tip
Using two layers of petals gives extra depth and makes the sunflower more interesting.

TIME: 30 minutes
DESIGNER: Elizabeth Moad

Burning Bright

Send a message of peace and goodwill at Christmas with this simple yet striking quilled candle design that's so easy to make from loosely coiled red and cream paper.

TIME: 30 minutes
DESIGNER: Lesley Price

Top Tip
Remove any unwanted specks of red glitter from the card with a small, dry paintbrush.

1 Make six loose coils from cream paper and pinch them in three places to form triangles. Stick half a length of red to the end of another half of orange. Starting with the orange, coil around the quilling tool. Allow the coil to unravel a little then fix the end of the red paper down. Pinch into a tear-drop.

2 Mount olive green card, 5cm x 11cm, onto a slightly larger piece of pale green, then silver mirror card, leaving a 3mm border. Attach a 7cm strip of 1cm wide double-sided tape down the centre. Arrange the cream triangles onto the tape in a candle shape. Fix the red quilled 'flame' with PVA glue.

3 Lightly shake fine red glitter over the quilling to cover the tape beneath and tap off excess. Stick onto the card blank. Thread red organza ribbon through a slit in the spine and knot at the front. Stick a metal greeting in the bottom right corner.

Wonderful Wirework

Create glittering shaped motifs or clips to provide the perfect finishing touch

Craft wire now comes in a rainbow of colours, and can be enhanced even further with beads and charms. Available in spools or loose coils, the basic rule is the higher the gauge, the finer the wire. There are also many handy gadgets available, such as peg boards that you can wrap your wire around to make instant shapes.

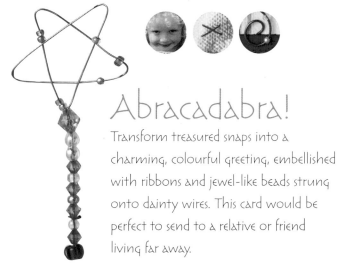

Abracadabra!

Transform treasured snaps into a charming, colourful greeting, embellished with ribbons and jewel-like beads strung onto dainty wires. This card would be perfect to send to a relative or friend living far away.

1 Trace lightly around each template segment with a pencil onto assorted coloured papers and photographs. Cut each piece out using scissors or a paper trimmer. Don't worry about any visible lines as all the edges will be distressed with ink or sandpaper.

2 Trim purple card, 13.5cm square, and textured pink paper, 15cm square. Use a black ink-pad to wipe over the edges of each piece of paper. Use medium grade sandpaper to distress the edges of all the photographs.

3 Position the block template over the purple square and secure with low-tack tape. Stick each element with double-sided tape, using the template as a placement guide.

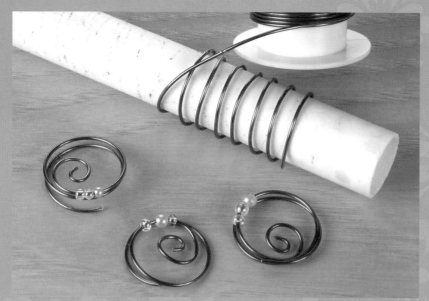

6 Find the middle of the wire and begin wrapping around the pegs. Twist the ends three times to secure. Feed eleven assorted beads onto both wire tails. Stitch one end through the last bead, then the other to secure the wand handle.

4 Wrap some 18 gauge pink wire around a plastic tube. Squeeze the wraps together to keep the coil nice and tight. Cut off two curls and shape into an attractive spiral using needle-nose pliers, by gripping one end and turning the wire with your other hand. Pass three beads onto each coil.

7 Trim away excess wire, then sew the wand to the card using a sharp needle and thread. Secure workings on the back with tape. To decorate, make crosses on the little square and attach ribbon using a stapler loaded with pink staples.

Top Tip

The finer gauge wires are perfect for problem hands as they are easy to shape. For safety, wire snips are a must as they always flick the cut ends away from your eyes

5 Use a wire peg board to make the magic wand. Position five pegs on the board in a star motif. Cut 30cm of 26 gauge pink wire and thread with seven seed beads.

8 Slide the wire clips onto the top right and bottom left corners. Using double-sided tape, mount pink paper to the the front of a folded 15cm square pink blank. Mount the decorated panel on top using 3D sticky foam pads.

1 Pass 50cm silver craft wire through a ribbler to give it an attractive wavy appearance, then use a peg board to form a frame with it as shown. Curl the ends into spirals at the top with pliers. Place the frame on a turquoise blank, 14cm square, and pierce the card with a needle under each corner. Use fine monofilament beading thread to secure the frame.

2 Form a scroll shape from pink wire and fix to the blank as before. Layer scraps of green ribbon and attach a flower sequin and bead on a safety pin. Using glue dots, add a shell heart with a twist of ribbon, and a paper scrap with kisses. Fix the ribbon inside the frame.

3 Punch a small hole at the top left of the card. Pass several strands of turquoise and silver thread through the hole, tie lightly and add a dab of glue to secure the threads. Use a textured insert if you wish.

Curly Wurly

Take a few twirls of wire and twist them to make a pretty frame or a scroll to go with a ribbon collage, for a beautiful and unusual greeting design.

Top Tip

When attaching chiffon ribbon, hide the glue dots behind the decorations.

TIME: 20 minutes

DESIGNER: Glennis Gilruth

Pretty Posy

Make a delicate feathery bouquet from coiled wire decorated with flower beads and a splendid marabou feather – a spectacular card that's sure to impress!

TIME: 25 minutes
DESIGNER: Jill Alblas

Top Tip
Wrap this card in pretty tissue paper instead of an envelope. Tie with a ribbon to match the colour used on the card.

1 Cut wire mesh, 7cm square, and stick narrow double-sided tape down one side. Bend the mesh into a cone and press very firmly onto the tape so that it holds its shape. Trim the excess with sharp scissors, then wrap ribbon around the cone and tie in a bow.

2 Press narrow double-sided tape down the back and fix it near the base of a tall card blank. Put a little glue down the centre of a marabou feather and position it so the end is inside the cone. Cut three sections of wire, 10cm long, coil the ends around a pen and thread each one with a flower bead.

3 Apply glue to the back of each bead and to the tip and coil of the wire. Position the flowers inside the cone vase over the feather. When you are happy with the way they look press the flowers down onto the card.

Star Turn

Combine beads with coiled wire, ribbons and stars to create a show-stopping card with real glitz – perfect for a special celebration.

Top Tip
If you're short of time, omit the beading and simply use a square of card in its place. The greeting would then take about 20 minutes to make.

TIME: One hour, 20 minutes
DESIGNER: Jill Alblas

1 Use half cross stitch to sew a 13-bead square of blue rocailles onto white embroidery fabric. Cut out the panel, leaving a 2cm border all the way round. Trim a 3.5cm square from a tall card blank, 2.5cm down from the centre top. Tape the beaded fabric on the back of the cut-out square.

2 Fold 20cm of organza ribbon in half and using tiny glue dots, stick it at an angle across the beading so the loop comes just below the top of the blank. Repeat with narrow satin ribbon but adhere it at a slightly different angle.

3 Coil 50cm each of silver and blue wire around a pen. Glue the spirals onto the card blank positioning their tops where the loops of ribbon overlap. Fix a silver and a gold star in place to hide the top of the wire using glue dots. Stick a star at the bottom of each spiral and add a few more in a random pattern over the card.

Angel Face

Create a pretty turquoise angel greeting embellished with matching beaded wirework as a simple and highly effective finishing touch.

Top Tip

You could make your own angel embellishment using polymer clay. See page 60 for inspiration on using this material.

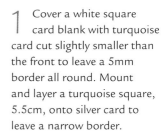

TIME: 30 minutes
DESIGNER: Caroline Blanchard

1 Cover a white square card blank with turquoise card cut slightly smaller than the front to leave a 5mm border all round. Mount and layer a turquoise square, 5.5cm, onto silver card to leave a narrow border.

2 Fix the layered turquoise panel to the centre of the blank using 3D sticky foam pads. Add your greeting underneath with rub-on lettering, or by drawing it on the card by hand.

3 Stick a small angel embellishment to the turquoise panel, closer to the top. Thread a few beads on a length of 18 gauge turquoise wire, and coil in a random pattern as shown. Attach to the card with PVA glue which will dry clear.

Trim the Tree

This eyecatching festive greeting features a Christmas tree decorated with coiled wire against a rich mulberry background.

1 Stick purple card onto the front of a white square blank, cut 5mm smaller all round. Mount a 5.5cm purple square onto plum card and trim to make a border. Fix this panel to the middle of the blank, using 3D sticky foam pads.

2 Add the words for your festive greeting vertically along the right edge of the panel with rub-on lettering, or draw it on by hand. Cut out a long triangle shape from plum card, and a small pot and star from green card.

3 Stick the Christmas tree, pot and star together, and fix to the central panel with double-sided tape. Cut and curl a length of 18 gauge purple wire in a rough zigzag shape to fit over the tree shape as shown, and glue down with PVA glue.

Top Tip
Embellish the curled wire further by adding beads, which will look like bauble decorations.

TIME: 30 minutes
DESIGNER: Caroline Blanchard

Criss Cross

Weave strips of co-ordinating paper to create a pretty background for a wire flower coiled from sparkling silver wire and embellished with a glass bead.

TIME: 45 minutes
DESIGNER: Jo Gratwick

Top Tip
Use the point of a needle to help weave the strips of paper into position if you find it fiddly without.

1 Fold A4 textured cream card in half and trim 6cm from the base. Snip 13, 2cm and 1cm strips, from pink and white pearlescent paper, in various shades and widths. Fix tape to a cutting mat sticky side uppermost. Place six strips side by side, their tops on the tape. Weave the other strips horizontally, under and over them.

2 Turn the design over, check you have a tight weave, then cover the back with tape to secure. Trim to 9.5cm square, mount onto brown card and fix to the centre of the cream blank.

3 Wind silver-coloured wire 16 times around a narrow metal ruler or lolly stick, and remove. Thread more wire through the coil, through a clear glass bead and back down the outside of the coil. Twist the ends with round-nosed pliers to secure, and use to make the stem. Fan out the petals, then stick to the card with a glue dot.

Thank you

Floral Thanks

Twist pink wire into a flower shape using a wire peg board to make a stunning decoration for a card, finished off with a paper flower centre.

Top Tip
A wire peg board is ideal for repeat pattern projects like Christmas cards and wedding stationery.

TIME: 45 minutes
DESIGNER: Melanie Hendrick

1 Design a simple flower shape you can map out with pegs on a wire peg board. Cut 90cm of 26 gauge pink wire. Leaving a 10cm tail at each end, wrap it around first the middle peg then an outside one to make a petal. Repeat until you have created all the petals for your flower and gently lift it off the board.

2 Using the wire tail, stitch between the petals, then through the centre hole to secure, repeating for each petal. When you reach the end, twist the leftover lengths together to make a stem. Shape the petals by stretching the loop with needle-nosed pliers, then opening it up about halfway along.

3 Attach a paper flower and brad to hide the untidy ends in the centre. Decorate the front of the card using torn paper and card strips. Attach the wire flower with tacky glue and leave to dry. Print a little tag greeting on the computer and attach to the stem with sticky pads.

From The Heart

Curl thick silver wire into a pretty heart shape and decorate with different size beads attached to thin wire to make a subtle and sophisticated greeting.

TIME: 20 minutes

DESIGNER: Emma Beaman

Top Tip

Using different sizes and colours of beads enhances the attractive asymmetrical feel of this design.

1 Fold white hammer-finish card into a 13cm square blank. Tear maroon paper, 9.5cm square, and red paper, 9cm square and stick them together. Cut 30cm of thick silver wire, then bend in the middle to form the heart's tip. Using pliers, coil one of the ends into a spiral on the inside of the heart shape. Repeat with the other end to match. Tweak the wire as you go to form the heart shape.

2 Cut a long length of thin wire and where the heart spirals meet, wrap it around several times to secure. Continue winding the wire around the coils and thread beads as you go.

3 Make the bead pattern random, twisting the wire to keep them firm. When complete, position onto the maroon square and make several pin pricks through the paper. Attach the heart to the background with wire. Stick the square centrally on the front of the card.

Stamping Out

Create beautiful cards in minutes by stamping them with a simple image

Anyone who has fond memories of creating potato-print pictures will love the variety of rubber stamps now available. There are so many designs, from traditional to funky and cute to chic, which can be applied swiftly using ink-pads. They take the craft a few steps further than potato printing ever did! You can also add a further dimension by colouring your motif afterwards with paints or pencils.

Floral Tribute

Flowers are the perfect gift when you want to express a sentiment, but just can't find the right words. Although this project looks complicated, it only involves stamping, colouring and cutting to achieve the finished result.

You will need

Flower Border stamp

Flower Bouquet stamp

Large and small butterfly stamp

Aubergine and leaf green ink-pads

Transparent crystal (holographic) embossing powder,

Ornamental corner bracket punch

Gold pen or gold leafing pen

White and lilac glitter card

Double-sided tape

Foam pads

Craft glue

Lilac flower, plain lilac and white paper

Assorted coloured pencils

Mini tag embellishments

Wedding hanging rod embellishments

Gold embroidery thread

Lilac organza ribbon

TIME: 15 minutes

PROJECT DESIGNER: Dorothy Walsh

1 Cut A4 lilac glitter card lengthwise, 11cm. Score and fold in the centre to make a side-fold blank. Trim lilac flower paper, 10cm x 14cm, and plain white card, 9cm x 13cm.

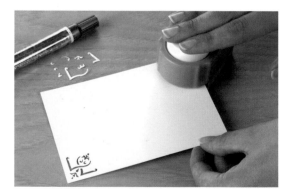

2 Push out diagonally opposite corners of the white card with the ornamental bracket punch, and edge all round with gold pen. Ink the flower border stamp with the aubergine pad and print diagonally across the white card towards the un-punched corners. Colour the image using pencils.

3 Ink the flower bouquet stamp with the aubergine pad and imprint three times onto a separate white card. Colour the whole of the first image, only the flowers on the second, and just one large bloom from the centre on the third. Use the same shades throughout.

Top Tip
Using a leafing pen on your projects really adds that extra special touch. The grooved bullet tip is ideal for creating straight edges, and adding highlights to your stamped images.

4 Using a sharp craft knife over a cutting mat, cut out the first bouquet, and the coloured flowers from the other two. Stick the individual shapes onto the corresponding blooms on the main stamped image, using 3D sticky foam pads. Fix the bouquet onto the main white card, placing it centrally over the previously stamped row of flowers.

6 Glue the centres of three large butterflies together to create a layered effect. Repeat with the small butterflies. Attach the insects to the main white card next to the bouquet of flowers using foam pads.

7 Fasten the white card to the middle of the patterned pink paper, and then onto the centre of the lilac glitter card with double-sided tape. Tie a bow around the stems of the flower bouquet using gold thread.

5 Ink the butterfly stamps with the laurel leaf pad and press onto white paper. Emboss the image using the holographic powder and a heat tool. Cut out both butterflies. Repeat three times.

8 Attach a small tag with lilac organza ribbon to the gold wedding rod and stick this vertically to the folded left side of the card, using craft glue. Line the inside of the blank with lilac paper to finish.

1 Take a green brush marker pen and colour in the stems on a long-stemmed triple flower stamp. Take a pink brush marker and outline the shape of the blooms on the stamp. Print an image of all three flowers out onto a piece of yellow card, 8cm x 9.5cm.

2 Using water-colour pencils, colour the stamped flower shapes in pink with a hint of yellow. Use a damp, fine paintbrush to blend the two shades and create the effect of a watercolour painting.

3 Colour the edges of the yellow card with yellow brush marker and mount the panel onto the front of a pink square card blank using 3D sticky foam pads.

Full Bloom

Discover the lovely subtle effects you can achieve from brush marker pens and water-colour pencils with rubber stamps. They're great fun to use, too.

Top Tip

Soften the edge of this simple card by tying a yellow ribbon around the spine ending in a bow. Fix inside the card with a sliver of double-sided tape.

TIME: 20 minutes
DESIGNER: Elizabeth Moad

Egg Hunt

The stamped image on this pretty pink Easter card was clear embossed before being coloured in, and mounted on gingham paper and sheer ribbon.

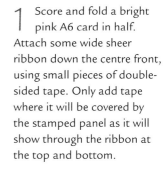

Top Tip

When you press the inked stamp onto the paper, be careful not to rock it. Press firmly and evenly, then lift directly off the paper.

TIME: 35 minutes

DESIGNER: Tracey Daykin-Jones

1 Score and fold a bright pink A6 card in half. Attach some wide sheer ribbon down the centre front, using small pieces of double-sided tape. Only add tape where it will be covered by the stamped panel as it will show through the ribbon at the top and bottom.

2 Stamp the image using black ink onto white linen-effect card and clear emboss. Use water-colour paints or pencils to colour the girl's dress, hair, eggs and basket. Leave to dry.

3 Trim and mount onto pink gingham paper then silver card, using double-sided tape. Attach to the main card with tape and embellish by adding a tiny gem stone to each corner using diamond glaze glue.

1 Ink up a background stamp with a repeating pattern using a multi-coloured blue ink-pad, and stamp it all over a strip of white card, 5.5cm wide. Trim to fit the length of a pearlescent turquoise blank.

2 Layer the stamped card onto blue card, 1cm wider, and use double-sided tape to mount this panel on the card blank towards the left-hand side. If applicable, decorate the centre of each stamped motif with some turquoise glue or a paint dot and leave to dry.

3 Use a black ink-pad to print your chosen greeting stamp onto the bottom right-hand corner of your card or draw on directly by hand. Add a blue, flat-backed crystal below the wording to finish.

Thinking of You

Special Thoughts

Make a card for a friend who's moved away to let them know they're in your thoughts. This cheerful design is suitable for any simple repeating pattern or colour scheme.

Top Tip
You don't need an occasion for every card, why not send one just because you want to!

TIME: 30 minutes
DESIGNER: Julie Hickey

Daisy Chain

Create a greeting in sunny shades of orange and yellow with a simple flower silhouette detail as a lovely reminder for someone of happy times shared together.

Top Tip
This subtle card can easily be adapted to include a message of your choice.

TIME: 15 minutes
DESIGNER: Julie Hickey

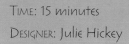

1 Cover a piece of white card with a striped background using a background stamp or similar, and a multi-coloured orange ink-pad. Leave to dry.

2 Ink up a tall thin daisy stamp with black ink and stamp this over the orange background. Trim the white card to size and layer onto orange card, leaving a 0.5cm border all the way round.

3 Cut a tall thin card blank from pearlescent coral card. Mount the stamped flower panel onto the top half of the blank, using double-sided tape and making the top and side edges equal.

1 Cut plaid paper the length of a card blank and two-thirds its width, then attach to the card with double-sided tape. Trim a piece of white card, 10cm square, and use a baby stamp to print an image in black or charcoal ink.

2 Colour the image with pink brush marker pen and dot with glitter glue. Once dry, mount onto pink and then silver mirror card, before fixing to the centre with sticky foam pads. Stamp a message next to the image and add small punched dots down the right edge.

3 For the tag, punch a large shape from white card and mount onto textured pink card, using double-sided tape. Make a small hole and thread with pink ric-rac ribbon.

4 Stamp teddy, dummy and rattle images using the same ink as before. Colour with brush markers and dot with glitter glue.

Baby Days

Celebrate a new addition to the family with this cute stamped greeting made using simple stamping techniques and a bright plaid background paper.

Top Tip
Store your ink-pads upside down to get the maximum life from them.

TIME: 40 minutes
DESIGNER: Wendy Horrod

Shell Out

This simple but effective rubber stamped card is perfect for a summer birthday and is created using two pretty shell images stamped all over orange mulberry paper.

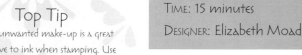
TIME: 15 minutes
DESIGNER: Elizabeth Moad

1 Using dark brown ink, stamp three shell shapes onto cream card and punch or cut out with a craft knife to make three small squares. Tear orange mulberry paper to fit the front of a brown card blank, painting a line with a wet paintbrush first to make tearing easier.

2 Stamp more shell motifs all over the orange mulberry paper using different shades of ink. To create a lighter design, print onto scrap paper first. Stick the finished piece to the front of the card.

3 Wrap yellow ribbon around the front and tie in a knot at the top. Attach the three cream shell squares, in a row. If you wish, add a greeting instead of the middle square.

Glitter Bug

This pretty card made from soft iridescent shades of lilac and white card stamped with a delicate butterfly image, is quick and easy to make, and sure to make a big impression!

1 Cut white card, 15cm x 21cm and fold in half to make a blank. From scraps of purple card, trim three rectangles measuring 5.5cm x 4.5cm, 8cm x 4cm and 10cm x 2cm.

2 With a small piece of sponge, apply white acrylic paint to a butterfly stamp and carefully print the image onto each strip of purple card. Don't worry if you can't fit the image onto the strip perfectly – it looks more interesting if only part of the butterfly is showing.

3 Once dry, arrange the purple rectangles on the white card blank. When you are happy with the way they look, use 3D sticky foam pads to attach them. Finish off by adding three lilac iridescent sequins down each butterfly's body.

Top Tip
Clean your stamps with a sponge and warm water straight after use. Don't immerse in water as this could loosen the rubber from the mount.

TIME: 15 minutes
DESIGNER: Jane Kharade

East Meets West

Rich colours and oriental patterns provide the basis for this charming greeting which features two gold embossed motifs and a stunning red, white and gold colour scheme.

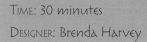

Top Tip
Buying sets of unmounted rubber stamps can save money, but be prepared to spend more time on preparing them for use.

TIME: 30 minutes
DESIGNER: Brenda Harvey

1 Fold an A5 sheet of red card in half and cover the front with patterned Japanese paper. Stamp a Japanese lady design onto white card, sprinkle with gold embossing powder and heat.

2 Trim the edges with deckle-edged scissors, layer onto gold card and punch two small holes at the top and the bottom. Thread red satin ribbon through each pair of holes and tie in place, trimming the ends neatly.

3 Attach the Japanese lady panel to the card blank, using 3D sticky foam pads. Follow the same basic process from step 1 using a flower stamp to make a second small square panel and fix it to the bottom right-hand corner of the card.

Pulling Punches

These handy gadgets take the effort out
of creating paper designs and achieve a
highly professional finish

Cutting out shapes for cardmaking can be awkward
and time-consuming, which is why the huge variety
of punches available are a real boon to crafters.
They work like a hole punch and can be used on
paper and card, to create stars, flowers, circles and
much more. There are even varieties for rounding
off corners.

Daisy Daisy

This would make a great card to send to a
teenager as it has a really young and funky
feel. Simply change the message and it could
become a thank you message, a party
invitation or a coming-of-age greeting.

happy birthday

1 Punch tiny daisies from yellow and orange card. Place randomly all over the front panel of the blank to create a background. Stick in place and leave to dry. It is easier to position the flowers by applying glue to the card, not the backs of the daisies.

2 Make a large daisy from pink card and curl the petals, using a pen or craft knife handle. Cut an orange square, 5.5cm, and a yellow square, 6cm. Use the corner rounder on both. Layer together with double-sided tape and fix to the blank with 3D sticky foam pads.

Top Tip

When layering the squares in step 2, remove part of the backing paper on the tape. Move the shapes around until in position, then remove all the tape.

3 Trim ribbon slightly larger than the blank. Tie another length around it and pull tight. Apply double-sided tape, slightly longer than the blank, where you want to place the ribbon. Attach firmly and trim to size. The tape will prevent fraying.

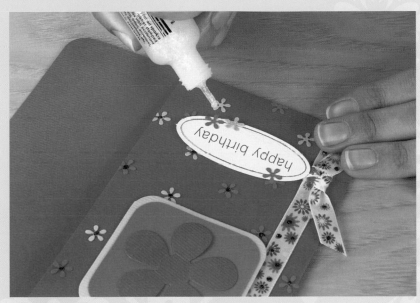

4 Decorate the oval message with some tiny punched-out daisies, and fix to the blank using 3D sticky foam pads. Decorate the centres of all the smallest flowers and the ribbon with glitter glue, and leave to dry.

6 Cut two small squares from orange card and two slightly smaller ones from yellow. Layer together with double-sided tape, as described in step 5. Punch small pink daisies to fill the centre of each one and fix using tacky glue.

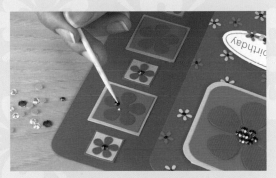

7 Space the layered squares down the right-hand panel of the blank. Start with the small ones at the top and bottom, and use a set square to ensure they are lined up correctly. Space the two larger squares and remaining small one as shown.

5 Cut two 4cm squares from yellow card, and two slightly smaller ones in orange. Layer together using double-sided tape. Punch a flower from pink card to fill the centre of each one, and stick in place with tacky glue.

8 Add crystals in the centres of the daisies – one for the smallest and three on the medium ones. The large daisy on the front panel has seven crystals that form a flower shape in the middle. It's easier to apply glue to the blank, not the crystals.

Secret Garden

Create a reminder of a beautiful garden in high summer with this gorgeous flower trellis card, made using easy punching and stencilling techniques.

TIME: 50 minutes

DESIGNER: Emma Beaman

1 Cut red card, 11cm x 27cm and fold in half lengthways. Using a strip of scrap card dipped into ivory acrylic paint, stencil on a lattice pattern as shown in the photo, then leave to dry. Mount the card onto the lower section of a blue, 14cm square blank, covering 10cm. Trim off the excess around the edges.

2 Punch out lots of flower shapes using different punches and coloured card. Take some of the blooms and paint the tip of each petal with coloured ink-pads. Brush them on gently to get a soft effect or use a circular dauber to add a coloured centre. Cut out small leaf shapes from green paper.

3 Arrange the flowers and leaves across the front and back of the blank, then fix in place. Some flowers may have loose petals that you can fold upwards a little to add depth. Trim any overhanging petals. Add diamond gems for detail.

Country Style

Use gingham patterned paper and quilling papers to recreate the look of pretty jampot covers waiting to go on delicious homemade fruit jams.

TIME: 50 minutes

DESIGNER: Susan Niner Janes

Top Tip

When sewing onto card, prick holes with a pin or needle first, using a ruler for a straight line. Then sew through these holes.

1 Trim white card, 20cm square. Score and fold in half. Trim yellow gingham paper to 2.5cm x 21cm, using zig-zag edgers down one side. Fix down the right of the blank, zig-zags inward. Add zig-zag rub-down stitching along the gingham border and a line of running stitch, 1cm from the card fold. Fix blue and yellow gingham paper to white card and punch three, 4cm circles. Cut three, 5cm circles with zig-zag edgers.

2 Snip green quilling strips in half for the stems and punch six hearts for the leaves. Glue onto the small gingham circles at an angle. Punch contrasting 1cm flowers and fix at the stalk tops. Punch tiny circles for the centres. Attach small gingham circles to the pinked backing discs using 3mm 3D sticky foam pads.

3 Wrap 3mm quilling paper snugly around the raised circles, gluing a 1cm overlap. Make three paper bows and glue. Fix discs on the card in a line, spaced evenly.

1 Score and fold pale pink A5 textured card in half to give a tall, narrow blank. Attach 15cm pink organza ribbon with double-sided tape, running vertically down the front from the top right-hand corner.

2 Punch two circles from pink card and one from green card, and attach them to the ribbon with PVA glue. Top them with daisies punched from a selection of pretty scrapbooking papers and vellum, glued on in a random pattern.

3 To complete the card, add small flat-backed crystals in a variety of colours in the centre of some of the flowers. Leave to dry. For an interesting effect, put two layers of punched flowers together – one patterned and one vellum.

Lovely Bunch

Flowers are always well received, making this an ideal card when time is short. It's decorated with flowers punched from different scrapbooking papers.

Top Tip
Sharpen your punches by punching through several layers of kitchen foil – use the foil shapes on a design afterwards!

TIME: 25 minutes

DESIGNER: Tracey Daykin-Jones

In Bloom

Our pretty cherry blossom greeting mounted on a lilac card blank can be made in minutes from materials you already have in your workbox.

TIME: 15 minutes
DESIGNER: Glennis Gilruth

1 Cut lilac card and fold in half to make a blank. Draw curved 'branches' on scraps of pink paper and cut using a sharp craft knife over a cutting mat. Arrange on the lilac blank and glue down. Cover the joins with a pink chiffon bow.

2 Punch ten small flowers from pink pearl paper. Arrange along the branches on the blank and glue in place. Add a self-adhesive red gem in the centre of each one.

3 Use a punch wheel or a leaf stamp to cut out tiny leaves to go next to each flower from a strip of lime green card. Perforate the middle of each leaf with pin marks for the veins. Alternatively, use a bone folder to score. Arrange next to the flowers and stick in place.

Ice Cool

This funky festive greeting will put you in the mood for making your own beautiful cards this year. You can adapt this quick design to suit another motif or colour.

1 Fold an A5 turquoise pearlescent card in half lengthways, scoring along the crease first to stop it from cracking. Punch out a large snowflake shape from white card, and set a self-adhesive crystal sticker in the centre to decorate it.

2 Stamp a seasonal greeting onto white card, using a permanent dye ink-pad in turquoise. Trim with deckle-edged scissors and then layer onto silver mirror card. Attach across the bottom right corner of the blank with double-sided tape.

3 Stick the large punched snowflake in place with a 3D sticky foam pad. Finish off your card by gluing white and silver confetti snowflakes and stars randomly across the background.

Top Tip
Use plain card instead of pearlescent and highlight areas with fine glitter powder.

TIME: 30 minutes
DESIGNER: Brenda Harvey

In a Pear Tree

Create a contemporary Christmas design using punched oak leaves and a real twig from the garden tied with a festive red ribbon.

Top Tip
Use rub-on lettering or print by hand if you don't use a computer.

TIME: 50 minutes
DESIGNER: Brenda Harvey

1 Take a tall white blank and mount layers of red, white and gold mirror card on it, using double-sided tape. Punch 24 green oak leaves and attach with sticky foam pads in a circular tree shape.

2 Cut a partridge from gold mirror card, using the template on page 254. Add detail using a black permanent marker pen. Stick to the tree with double-sided tape. Tie red satin ribbon round a twig and glue on as the trunk.

3 Trim a small pot from gold mirror card, add two thin strips of red and fix to the bottom of the tree with 3D sticky foam pads. Print the text from a computer, tear the edges and attach to the design on a layer of red.

... and a partridge in a pear tree...

Iced Gem

It only takes a few pretty motifs, like these punched silver flowers decorated with liquid pearl dots to make a gorgeous seasonal greeting that your friends will love.

TIME: One hour

DESIGNER: Françoise Read

1 Cut a Christmas tree from light turquoise paper. Decorate with small, printed jade flowers. Sponge the edges with jade ink. Attach the motif to a silver background card, 9.5cm x 14.5cm, and then to a light turquoise panel, 10cm x 15cm. Add a silver brad in each corner and mount onto white folded card, 11.5cm x 18cm, using sticky foam pads.

2 Punch three flowers from silver card, decorate with liquid pearl dots and stick down the middle of the tree using 3D sticky foam pads. Punch smaller flowers from light turquoise paper and fix silver circles in the middle. Dot around card. Cut out a vase shape and attach using sticky foam pads. Add a white bow.

3 Punch out a tag, mount on silver card and tear round. Add a silver punched flower as before, tie on a ribbon. Fix to the card and write a message in silver pen.

Frame It!

Create a suitable backdrop for a host of brightly coloured punched daisies by making a matching striped frame and fix it to your card with 3D sticky foam pads.

Top Tip
Draw round a 5cm square template and cut using a craft knife if you don't have a square aperture punch.

TIME: 30 minutes
DESIGNER: Brenda Harvey

1 Use a 5cm square punch to create the frame on this design. Punch out a square from blue striped card then trim the frame border on all four sides, to a width of 1.5cm with a sharp craft knife. Attach to a turquoise pearlescent card blank, 13.5cm square when folded, with 3D sticky foam pads.

2 Punch a series of different flowers from turquoise and lime green card. Add a contrasting centre to each one cut with a single-hole punch. Arrange the blooms within the frame and stick using 3D sticky foam pads.

3 To finish, punch a heart shape from lime green card and fix it to the top left-hand corner of the frame with a 3D sticky foam pad.

Weaving About

Create traditional designs with a modern twist, using ribbons in different styles and designs

Ribbon weaving is an easy technique that adds a wonderful tactile quality to your cards. Simply cut into lengths and weave together to create a panel. The weaving can be stretched over a piece of card or made to fit behind a square or shaped aperture. Experiment by adding fancy yarns with the ribbons, or weave diagonally to create different effects.

New Arrival

This pretty design uses a woven ribbon panel as a pocket for a tag, which is embellished with more ribbons to bring the different elements together. You can change the colour scheme to pink for a girl, or try other, contrasting shades.

You will need

White hammered card

2cm wide, blue gingham ribbon;

2.5cm and 6mm wide
sheer pale blue ribbon;

1.8cm wide pale blue ribbon;

2cm wide sheer baby feet ribbon;

4mm wide white ribbon;

Double-sided tape and stapler

Baby blue ink-pad

Pastel blue baby buttons: one 1.3cm
and one 2.3cm

TIME: 35 minutes

PROJECT DESIGNER: Dorothy Wood

2 Fix double-sided tape down both short edges. Remove the backing paper from one section and fasten 12cm lengths of different ribbon alongside each other.

1 Trim white card, 10.5cm x 6cm, and apply double-sided tape along the top edge on the reverse side. Cut enough 8cm lengths of gingham, pale blue, sheer and baby feet design ribbons to fit across the rectangle. Remove the backing paper and stick the ribbons side-by-side.

3 Flip the panel, fold every second short ribbon length over and use the first long strip to hold the short ones down. Stick the end on the reverse side. Continue weaving the remaining long lengths across the card.

Top Tip
If you are struggling to get the ribbons to fit exactly across the card rectangle, just cut it slightly longer or shorter and adjust the base card to suit

4   Fix a length of double-sided tape across the bottom side and fold the ends of the long ribbon to the reverse side. Apply more tape down the bottom edge and repeat for the short ribbon.

5   Trim the main card blank from white hammered card, 10.5 x 12cm, and run the edges through a baby blue ink-pad. Fasten the woven panel on the front, using double-sided tape along the bottom and short edges, to form a pocket.

6   Snip a tag shape, 5.5cm x 9cm, from white hammered card. Rub the baby blue ink-pad over the textured side to colour it and then run the edges through the pigment as well.

7   Wrap a 30cm length of baby feet sheer ribbon around the tag lengthways. Cut two, 15cm sections of gingham and narrow, sheer, pale blue ribbon, and fold in half. Hold the ribbons at the top of the tag and secure with a stapler.

8   Thread narrow white ribbon through the pastel baby buttons and tie in a reef knot. Trim the ends at an angle and glue the smaller button to the tag, then the larger one onto the woven ribbon panel. Tuck the tag into the pocket.

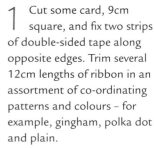

1 Cut some card, 9cm square, and fix two strips of double-sided tape along opposite edges. Trim several 12cm lengths of ribbon in an assortment of co-ordinating patterns and colours – for example, gingham, polka dot and plain.

2 Turn the card over and lay the ribbons across it, securing with the tape on the back. When covered, mount the panel centrally onto black card, 9.5cm square, then glue onto a pink card blank, 12cm square, with the ribbons running vertically.

3 Draw an asymmetric star shape on the back of iridescent effect paper. Cut the shape out with sharp scissors or a craft knife and fix to the top left-hand corner of the ribbon square with a 3D sticky foam pad.

Star Struck

Here's a simple yet effective design for a greeting using a single line of co-ordinating ribbons arranged vertically across the card.

Top Tip
You can vary the weight, texture, patterns and colours of ribbon used, but try to keep a common theme throughout.

TIME: 15 minutes
DESIGNER: Corinne Bradd

Handbags and Gladrags

Make this gorgeous girly greeting for a best friend to remind her of fun shopping trips you've shared. It's decorated with a cute handbag cut from pretty floral card.

TIME: 15 minutes
DESIGNER: Corinne Bradd

Top Tip
If your ribbon won't lie flat, iron gently, placing a clean cloth over the ribbon first to avoid scorching

1 Take a white A6 card blank and cover with a spotted paper, trimming the edges neatly. Trim a 2.5cm wide strip of co-ordinating diamond print paper and stick down the left-hand side, 1cm from the fold.

2 Use a small template to cut a rounded flap envelope from striped card. Score the folds and glue the sides together. Hold the flap down with a small 3D sticky foam pad and fix a small gingham ribbon bow over the flap on the outside. Snip a handbag shape from floral card and tie thin pink satin ribbon, 10cm long, around the handle.

3 Cut several more lengths of thin coloured ribbon, thread under the knot, fold over and secure by tying the pink ribbon over the top. Hold this in place with a dot of PVA glue. Fix the envelope and the bag onto the front of the card with 3D sticky foam pads.

1 Trim card, 14cm x 2cm, and apply a wide strip of double-sided tape to one side. Snip five sections of plain and striped grosgrain ribbon, 8cm long and stick under the corners of the wider pieces to form a point.

2 Place the ribbons in the middle of the card, fold the top 2cm over and tape down on the back. Fold the ends of the strip in and glue to a cream blank, 15cm square, so the centre section stands slightly proud of the card.

3 Fix the ribbons in place with a dab of glue. Fasten golden chocolate coins to the wider ends with an adhesive pad, and coloured buttons in co-ordinating colours to the narrower ribbons to create a row of medals.

Award Winner

Celebrate an important achievement by making a brilliant card decorated with medals using grosgrain ribbon, buttons and chocolate coins.

Top Tip

Since you can't buy single chocolate coins, you will have to buy a whole bag and eat the remainder. Or share them around if you must!

TIME: 15 minutes
DESIGNER: Corinne Bradd

Strip Tease

This delightful greeting is created from patterned papers in pretty shades of purple and lilac, and has co-ordinating ribbon threaded through slits cut down one side.

Top Tip

Use an insert for this card to hide the ribbon ends. Alternatively, stick a piece of card over the ribbon on the inside left.

TIME: 15 minutes
DESIGNER: Corinne Bradd

1 Score and fold A5 purple card to form an A6 blank. Trim lilac patterned paper, 9.5cm x 13.8cm and glue to the front. Fix darker patterned paper, 3cm x 13cm, down the right-hand side of the panel.

2 Draw two feint pencil lines, 1.5cm apart down the left side of the blank. Use a scalpel to cut an even number of slits between the marks, 1cm apart. Thread grosgrain and satin ribbon in and out of the cuts, and secure neatly on the inside with double-sided tape.

3 Snip a simple dragonfly shape from lilac pearlescent card. Bend the wings slightly and fix to the blank with 3D sticky foam tape. Decorate the body and wings with white pearlized 3D paint and allow to dry.

Fun Festoons

Brighten up someone's day with this colourful ribbon greeting. The ribbons are arranged in a fan shape and fixed behind a decorated card panel.

1 Cut cream card, 4cm square and mount onto lime green paper, 5cm square. Mount this onto cream card, leaving a 2mm border all round. Place double-sided tape on two adjacent sides of the square on the back.

2 Cut 11 or 12, 4cm lengths of assorted grosgrain ribbon. Snip a 'v' shape into one end of each to make a decorative tail. Fix the other ends to the tape on the back in the shape of a fan, on one corner of the card.

3 Fix the panel in the top left of a 10.5cm square card blank, so the tails fill the opposite corner. Snip a 'v' into both ends of striped grosgrain, 6cm long, twist and glue to the centre of the square. Add a co-ordinating flower gem on either side.

Top Tip
Loosely roll your ribbons and store in clear pots with lids. An ideal way to recycle old deli-tubs. Wash and dry thoroughly first.

TIME: 15 minutes
DESIGNER: Corinne Bradd

Patchwork Panel

Mix and match a wide variety of ribbons to create an eye-catching patchwork greeting. The ribbons are wrapped around strips of card then assembled on the card.

Top Tip
Never throw anything away: this card is a perfect way to use up ribbon ends and old scraps.

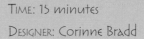

TIME: 15 minutes
DESIGNER: Corinne Bradd

1 Cut three card strips, 14cm x 2cm, and cover one side of each with wide double-sided tape. Snip 3.5cm lengths from 30–40 different ribbons in varying widths and patterns.

2 Position the ribbons across the tape on all three strips, covering the card completely and leaving tails at each end. Turn the strips over and fix the raw ends in place with double-sided tape on the back.

3 Score and fold in half a tall, pearlescent card blank in red or another strong colour. Stick one ribboned strip down the centre, 2cm from the top. Glue the other strips either side of the first, making the edges butt up close together to form a patchwork effect.

Woven Wonder

You can make a fantastic greeting by weaving lengths of co-ordinating ribbon together and setting them behind a decorative diamond card aperture.

Top Tip

Decorate an envelope to match the card. Take a piece of blue ribbon and fix it across the front of the envelope, attaching with double-sided tape under the flap at the back.

TIME: 15 minutes

DESIGNER: Corinne Bradd

1 Score and fold A4 lime green card into three. Using a template, draw a decorative diamond shape in the top half of the centre panel. Check the shape is still central when the card is folded and cut with a sharp craft knife over a cutting mat. Fix double-sided tape along one long edge of the diamond inside the card.

2 Place lengths of co-ordinating ribbon diagonally across the diamond, holding one end in place with the tape. When the whole of the aperture is covered, place double-sided tape along the two adjacent edges of the shape.

3 Weave ribbon across the diamond, fixing the ends in place with the tape. When the 'fabric' is complete, fasten the loose ends on the remaining side down, and stick the right-hand card flap down to cover the raw edges. Decorate the borders of the diamond with strips of zig-zag peel-off border.

Spot Check

Make a charming contemporary greeting using pink polka dot 'ribbon' you have stamped and cut from card, then glued in a flower shape. A lovely idea for every occasion.

TIME: 25 minutes
DESIGNER: Julie Hickey

Top Tip
You can reduce the amount of time it takes to make this card by covering card with ready-printed polka dot paper and using real spotted ribbon.

1 Stamp a pink dotted pattern across a strip of white card and leave to dry. Then do the same with a polka dot ribbon stamp using a pink ink-pad. Cut lengths of card 'ribbon' with a guillotine and bend eight pieces in half gently to form petals.

2 Arrange the petals in a flower shape on a square card blank and secure with double-sided tape. Stamp more of the pink dotted pattern onto white card, punch a circle and add a big pink brad. Fix in the flower centre.

3 Cut two more ribbons to form tabs down the right of the card, tape and decorate with glitter glue. Cut a message from card and emboss with circles. Edge the dotted panel with glitter glue.

Templates

All Templates on this page are 100%

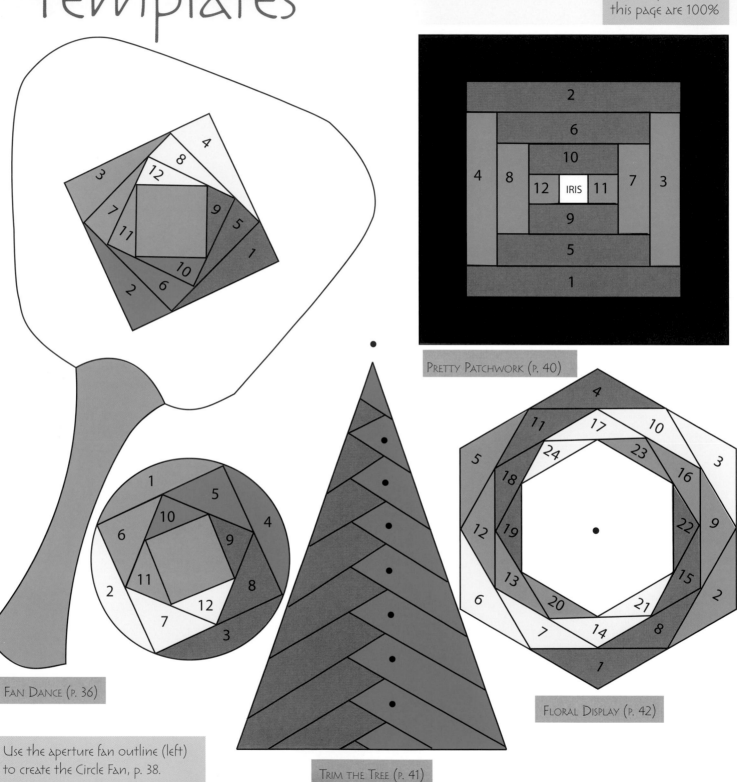

Pretty Patchwork (p. 40)

Fan Dance (p. 36)

Use the aperture fan outline (left) to create the Circle Fan, p. 38.

Trim the Tree (p. 41)

Floral Display (p. 42)

All Templates on this page are 50%, enlarge on a photocopier by 200%

HEART TO HEART (P. 92)

WRAPPED UP (P. 103)

PERFECT PENWORK (P. 84)

WARM WELCOME (P. 90)

WINTER WARMER (P. 94)

COFFEE TIME (P. 95)

FAIRY WISH (P. 107)

FAMILY TREE (P. 91)

OH CRUMBS (P. 93)

PRETTY PARCHMENT (P. 12)

ON THE WING (P. 17)

RETRO REVIVAL (P. 188)

MISTLETOE (P. 16)

Templates

All Templates on this page are 50%, enlarge on a photocopier by 200%

IN A PEAR TREE (P. 237)

RETAIL THEREPY (P. 118)

FAIRY CAKE (P. 184)

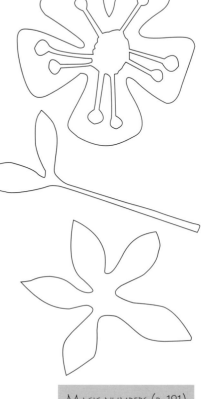

IN THE FRAME (P. 114)

BUNNIES AT PLAY (P. 189)

MAGIC NUMBERS (P. 191)

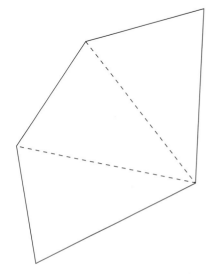

BIRDIE SONG (P. 174)

PICTURE PERFECT (P. 187)

LAZY DAISY (P. 186)

Where to buy?

Pink Lady (p. 12), Mistletoe (p. 16), Taste of Darjeeling (p. 24), Emerald City (p. 31), Eastern Promise (p. 34) Centagraph, 0800 328 5237 www.centagraph.co.uk *for parchment paper, embossing tools and inks, Poona tea bag papers, tile tea bag papers*

Floral Tribute (p. 216) The Stamp Store, 01229 834011 *for stamps*

On the Wing (p. 17), Holly Blue (p. 18) Impex, 0208 9000999, www.impexcreativecrafts. co.uk *for rocailles*; Cardcraft Plus, 01772 272572, www.cardcraftplus.co.uk, *for parchment*

Winter Wonderland (p. 19) Craftastic, Uckfield, 01825 766441 *for vellum, glitter, mirror card, ribbon*; Craft Barn, 01342 836097, www.craftbarn.co.uk *for Sizzix snowflake paddle punch*

Fan Dance (p. 36) Craft Central, 0161 980 0048, www.craftcentralltd.com *for Papermania Citrus Designer Papers - Colossal Paper Pack, Paper Cellar pearlescent turquoise and red card*

Pretty Patchwork (p. 40) Hobbycraft, www.hobbycraft.co.uk *for Aitoh Origami Paper: Kimono and Folk Art Design KM-1*

Trim the Tree (p. 41) Personal Impressions, 01787 375241, www.richstamp.co.uk *for JEJE Two-Tone Star Creative Paper*

Floral Display (p. 42) Hobbycraft, www.hobbycraft.co.uk *for Aitoh Colorwave Origami Paper*; Monoco Direct, www.monacodirect.co.uk *for Paper Shapers Kaleidopunch Foliage – Friendship*

Remembrance Day (p. 48) Lazertran Ltd, 01545 571149, www.lazrctran.com *for transfer paper*

Beach Comber (p. 52) Lazertran Ltd, 01545 571149, www.lazertran.com *for Lazertran inkjet paper*

Queen of Hearts (p. 60) Staedtler UK Ltd, 01443 237421, www.staedtler.co.uk *for Fimo*

Flower Power (p. 67) Staedtler (UK) Limited, 01443 237421 *for Fimo Soft polymer clay*

Merry Makes (p. 70) PDA Card and Craft, www.pdacardandcraft.co.uk *for card blanks*; The Craft Barn, 01342 836097, www.craftbarn.co.uk *for Makins clay*

Fond Memories (p. 72) PaperArts, 01453 886 038, www.paperarts.co.uk *for Bazzill Quartets cardstock (ruby slipper, sherbet, mocha, watermelon), Chatterbox Scrapbook Walls paper (20503), pastel chalk inks, brads*

Love Birds (p. 77) Laines Floral Art & Hobby Craft Shop, www.lainesworld.co.uk, *for Clear Choice stamps: Marriage (RL-CCS007)*

Funky Diva (p. 78) Calico Crafts, 01353 624100, www.calicocrafts.co.uk *for Making Memories Jelly Labels: Birthday 1, Rubber Stampede Chic (3752F)*

Home Coming (p. 80) Craftime, 01623 722828, www.craftime.co.uk

Retro Revival (p. 81) The Range, www.therange.co.uk *for elements ribbon*

Pet Shop Boys (p. 82), Cute Kitty (p. 83) www.stampeezee.co.uk *for Funstamps paw print (F-AA12), Hero Arts printer's lowercase alphabet stamps (LL762), Creative Impressions dog bone clips (85207)*

Bear Necessities (p. 84) Craft Creations 01992 781900 *for water-colour cards*; Calico Crafts, 01353 624100, www.calicocrafts.co.uk *for DecoArt Americana paints: bahama blue (DA255), petal pink (DA214), taffy cream (DA05), pistachio mint (DA253), deep periwinkle (DA212)*; Paper Arts, www.paperarts.co.uk *for Sizzix items, Making memories embellishment papers*; Wooden-It-Be-Lovely, 01296 748683, www.wooden-it-be-lovely.co.uk *for brushes*

Family Tree (p. 91), Heart to Heart (p. 92), Oh Crumbs! (p. 93), Coffee Time (p. 95) Calico Crafts, 01353 624100, www.calicocrafts.co.uk *for DecoArt Americana acrylic paints*

Winter Warmer (p. 94) www.wooden-it-be-lovely. co.uk *for products and workshops using this technique*

Folk Art (p. 96) Arty & Crafty Ltd, 0191 2189991 *for card and pom-pom trim*; John Lewis *for buttons, sequins, beads and bondaweb*; Ring-a-Rosie, 0191 2528874 *for fabrics*

Soft Centres (p. 105), Sew Cute (p. 106) John Lewis, www.johnlewis.com *for a selection of fabrics*

Beautiful Beading (p. 108) Trimcraft; www.trimcraft.co.uk for nearest stockist *for Mulberry mat stack, textured card mat stack, double-sided tape*; Lakeland Limited, 0153 9488100, www.lakelandlimited.co.uk *for turquoise craft wire*; Southfield Stationers, 0131 6544305, www.southfield-stationers.co.uk *for Tropical purple felt finish card, Still Violet paper*; Gutermann beads, 0208 5891640 for stockist information; www.millhill.com *for Mill Hill beads*; www.josayrose.com *for tiny sequins*

Lovely Lacé (p. 120) S for Stamps, 01355 570999, www.sforstamps.co.uk

In the Can (p. 136), Heart Throb (p. 140), Big Love (p. 141), Barrow Boy (p. 142), Secret Garden (p. 232), Coats Crafts UK, 01325 394241 *for Fiskars products*

Clever Togs (p. 137) Courtyard Crafts, 0151 3424216 *for QuickKutz baby set*

New Leaf (p. 143) www.sizzix.com *for nearest supplier*

Baby Steps (p. 138) Stamping Bug, www.stampingbug.com *for baby feet stamp*; American Crafts, www.americancrafts.com *for 12" double-sided paper*; One Purple Cow Ltd, 01784 740 442, www.onepurplecow.com *for Ricrac, Bazzill card, Doodlebug button assortment*

Touch of Frost (p. 150) Craft Barn, 01342 836097, www.craftbarn.co.uk *for vellum, ShapeBoss*;

Card Craft Plus 01772 272572, www.Cardcraftplus. co.uk *for Snowflake medallion stamp*

Charm School (p. 156) PaperArts, 01453 886 038, www.paperarts.co.uk *for Bazzill Quartets cardstock (mocha) and vibrant blue cardstock, white card blank*; Hobbycraft, 01452 384027, www.hobbycraft.co.uk *for Outline Stickers by Anita's (funky retro shapes; fab retro shapes; silver lines), blue chalk*

Gift Token (p. 160) PSW Print & Papers Ltd, 01527 853136 *for transparent gift stickers*

Check It Out (p. 163) The Craft Barn, 01342 836097 *for peel-offs and Peel Off's pens*

Mosaic Frame (p. 166) The Art of Craft, 01252 377677, www.art-of-craft.co.uk *for Starform stickers and Pergamano needle/pricking tool*

Let's Fly Away (p. 167) Topaz Crafts, www.topazcrafts.co.uk *for Dawn Bibby Designs butterfly peel-offs*

Heat Wave (p. 168) One Purple Cow Ltd, 01784 740 442, www.onepurplecow.com

True Blue (p. 172) 01732 762555 *for repositional Glue Dots* www.letraset.com/uk/craft *for Letraset snowflakes silver foil transfer*

Birdie Song (p. 174) 01535 616290 www.gluedotsuk.co.uk *for glue dots, Micro Dots, Micro Glitter, Magic Motifs, robin and ivy*

Scent with Love (p. 176) The Lavender People, 0121 2436067 *for dried lavender*

Four Seasons (p. 177) Design Objectives, 01202 811000, www.docrafts.co.uk *for snowflake stamp*

Pretty Posies (p. 178) The Craft Barn, 01342 836097, www.thecraftbarn.co.uk *for Hero Arts Angels in a Vase (E3086) stamp*; Paper Arts, 01453 886038, www.paperarts.co.uk *for Coluzzle cutting system*

Window Dressing (p. 179) The Craft Barn, 01342 836097, www.thecraftbarn.co.uk *for Anna Griffin Hydrangea (580H03), Penny Black Always (1970C) and Happy Definition*

Rain Dance (p. 180) Calico Crafts, 01353 624100, www.calicocrafts.co.uk *for DecoArt Americana Calypso Blue (DA 234) and Cool White (DA 240) acrylic paints,* Do Art, 0191 4605915, www.doart.co.uk *for Artcel tri-acetate or stencil film*

National Grid (p. 185), Lazy Daisy (p. 186) Pebeo, 0238 0901914/5, www.pebeo.com *for acrylic paints*; Kars, www.kars.biz *for cards and Aleene's acrylic paint*

Magic Numbers (p. 191) Hobbycraft stores, 0800 0272387 *for translucent paper, Making Memories charmed phrases*

Baby Steps (p. 138) Courtyard Crafts, 0151 3424216 (all materials)

Gardener's World (p. 192), Let's Twist Again (p. 196), Oriental Charm (p. 197), Wings of Love (p. 198), Winged Wonders (p. 199) Jane Jenkins Quilling Design, 01482 843721, www.janejenkins-quillingdesign.co.uk *for quilling*

papers and tools; Evie's Crafts, 01706 712489, www.eviescraftsltd.co.uk *for fringing tools*; Craft Creations Ltd, 01992 781900, www.craftcreations.co.uk *for blank card*; CraftWork Cards, 0113 2765713 *for shaped card blanks*; The Scrapbookhouse, 0870 7707717 *for Coastline umbrella striped paper*

Pretty Posy (p. 209) Homecrafts, 0116 2697733 *for mesh*; Kars, www.kars.biz *for flower beads*

Star Turn (p. 210) Impex, 0208 9000999, www.impexcreativecrafts.co.uk *for Rocailles*

Criss Cross (p. 213) The Paper Mill, 01539 564951, www.thepapermillshop.co.uk *for card*; Craftwork Cards, 01132765713, www.craftworkcards.co.uk *for paper strips*

From the Heart (p. 215) Hobbycraft, 0800 0272387, www.hobbycraft.co.uk *for silver jewellery wire, glass beads*

Full Bloom (p. 220) Centagraph, 0800 3285237 *for Hero Arts Fanciful Posies (LL923) stamp*

Egg Hunt (p. 221) Craft Addicts, 01270 875577 *for Penny Black So Eggciting (2599K) stamp*

Baby Days (p. 224) The Craft Barn, 01342 836097 *for new baby stamps and Zig brushables pens*

Glitter Bug (p. 226) Crafts of India, www.craftsofindia.co.uk *for sequins*

East Meets West (p. 227) www.roze.co.uk *for Washi papers,* Blade Rubber Stamps 020 78314123; www.bladerubberstamps.co.uk *for All Night Media Japanese stamp set (2412R)*

Daisy Daisy (p. 228) Craftwork Cards, 0113 2765713, www.craftworkcards.co.uk *for oval message, crystals, Crafts Too Tiny Daisy, corner punches*

Lovely Bunch (p. 234) Craftdee, 018582 414043, www.craftdee.co.uk *for Woodware Collection daisy punch*

In Bloom (p. 235) Letraset, 01233 624421 *for Letraline flex-a-tape*

Ice Cool (p. 236), In a Pear Tree (p. 237), Picture Perfect (p. 187) S for Stamps, 01355 570999, www.sforstamps.co.uk *for custom made stamps*

Iced Gem (p. 238) The Stamp Man, 01756 797048, www.thestampman.co.uk *for Woodware clear retro Christmas Elements (FRCL012)*; www.eksuccess.com *for EK Success tag, medium and small flower punches*

Frame It! (p. 239) Dream Crafts, 020 8873 2893, www.dreamcraftstore.co.uk *for EK Success medium folk heart punch (PSM84C) and Woodware large kikyou/petal punch (821-30)*; Natty Netty, www.nattynetty.co.uk *for Woodware mini daisy punch (NV32) and large daisy punch (NV16)*

Spot Check (p. 251) F W Bramwells, 01282 860388, www.bramwellcrafts.co.uk *for Hero Arts Polka Dot Ribbon, Tiny Jubilee Dots (C3085) stamps*; Craftwork Cards, 0113 2765713, www.craftworkcards.co.uk *for Tutti Frutti Textured Blox*

Index